P-38 LIGHTNING AT WAR

Joe Christy & Jeff Ethell

LONDON

IAN ALLAN LTD

Acknowledgements

A work of this kind is hardly possible without the aid of a great many people. The authors cannot adequately thank all those who helped, but we can dedicate this book to them.

So, we trust that you will approve of the use we made of your help, Ginny Fincik, and Maj Shirley Bach of the USAF 1361st Photo Squadron; and Wayne Pryor at Lockheed, James Knott of the Allison Division of General Motors, and General Ben Kelsey.

This book is also dedicated to Osamu Tagaya who unearthed Japanese records, and Arno Abendroth who delved into Luftwaffe files; to Bruce Hoy of the Air Museum, Papua, New Guinea; our fellow researchers in Australia, T. R. Bennett and Frank F. Smith; and to Dennis Glenn Cooper, Ira Latour, Wayne Sneddon, Ralph P. Willet, and William Carter.

It is also for Carl Bong, brother of America's Ace of Aces; authors Kenn C. Rust, Roger A. Freeman who opened his extensive P-38 file to us, and the generous Edward Jablonski, along with Mitch Mayborn, John Stanaway, Merle Olmsted, T. R. Bennett, and Glenn Bavousett. And for Ken Sumney and Emery J. Vrana.

Especially, it is dedicated to the ex-Lightning commanders and pilots who contributed: Oliver B. Taylor, John Tilley, Doug Canning, Hank Schneider, Carroll 'Andy' Anderson, Jack Lenox, Lee Carr, Sidney Inglet, Sterling Winn, Warren Campbell, George Laven, Art Beimdiek, Bill Hoelle, Frank Barnecott, George Fleckenstein, Jack Curtis, Downey Clinch, Guy Watson, Norm Jackson, Frank Lawson, Jack Fehrenbach, Tom Jones, Dick Burns, Revis Sirmon, Ben Mason, Ray Toliver, Robbie Robertson, Jules Hymel, Frank Shearin, Ross Humer, Richard Bracey, Hugh Bozarth, Jack Goebel, Carroll Knott, Harry Brown, Don Dessert, Nick Zinni, Jack Jones, Bob Margison, Carl Gardner, Sherrill Huff, Bill Caughlin, Francis Pope, Billy Broadfoot, John Stege, Erv Ethell, J. B. Woodson, George O. Doherty, Robert H. French, Noah Ray Tipton, James E. Kunkle, Fredric Arnold, D. A. Suddeth, Bob Woodard, and Royal Frey. Again, our sincere thanks...

Joe Christy and Jeff Ethell

First published 1978

ISBN 0 7110 0772 1

Design by Anthony Wirkus LSIAD

© J. Christy and J. L. Ethell 1978

Published by Ian Allan Ltd, Shepperton, Surrey, and printed in the United Kingdom by Ian Allan Printing Ltd

Contents

The following was originally printed in the US Army paper, *Stars and Stripes* in 1943, and was written by a B-17 gunner in North Africa. It was forwarded by ex-Liberator pilot, Fred Bowen, Canoga Park, California.

Oh, Hedy Lamarr is a beautiful gal
And Madeline Carroll is, too;
But you'll find, if you query, a different
   theory
Amongst any bomber crew.
For the loveliest thing of which one
   could sing·
(This side of the Heavenly Gates)
is no blonde or brunette of the
   Hollywood set,
But an escort of P-38s . . .

Sure, we're braver than hell; on the
   ground all is swell —
In the air it's a different story.
We sweat out our track through the
   fighters and flak;
We're willing to split up the glory.
Well, they wouldn't reject us, so
   Heaven protect us
And, until all this shooting abates,
Give us the courage to fight 'em — and
   one other small item —
An escort of P-38s.

Prelude: The Company

In February 1937 when the US Army Air Corps asked America's struggling aircraft industry to submit design proposals for a new 'interceptor', Lockheed Aircraft Corporation was a small company. Its cash on hand was approximately equal to one month's operating expenses; and its sole product, the twin-engined Electra, aimed at the feeder airline market, could claim a production run of less than 80 machines during the preceding three years.

Nevertheless, Lockheed made a bold response to the Air Corps' request, submitting drawings of an airplane so advanced that, if built, it would demand answers to engineering and aerodynamic questions for which no answers yet existed. Lockheed called the design 'Model 22'. The Air Corps would call it the P-38 Lightning.

'Model 22' represented the 22nd design proposed by Lockheed engineers since the company was founded 11 years earlier by Allen Lockheed, John Northrop, W. K. Jay and Fred Keeler. Eight of those designs had been produced for a total of 277 airplanes, 196 of which were the wooden Lockheeds, such as the famed Vegas, Orions, and Altairs.

In 1929 the company founders had sold out to a Detroit group, which in turn allowed Lockheed to slip into receivership as the commercial aircraft market dwindled during the Great Depression. Then, in 1932, company assets were purchased for $40,000 by a group brought together by investment banker Robert E. Gross (who had previously backed Lloyd Stearman in Wichita). These people originally included airline pioneer Walter Varney, Lloyd Stearman (who had sold out to United Aircraft three years earlier), Thomas F. Ryan III of Mid-Continent Air Lines, broker E. C. Walker, and Mr and Mrs Cyril Chappellet.

Gross also brought in engineer Hall Hibbard, who had begun his career with Stearman in 1927, after earning his degree at MIT. Hibbard was responsible for

Below: The 10-passenger Model 10 Electra, introduced in 1934, cruised at 185mph, and enjoyed immediate success with airline operators around the world.
/ Lockheed California Company

Above: Key executives who provided the foundation for Lockheed Aircraft Corporation were photographed together on 26 July 1934. Left to right: Lloyd Stearman, Robert Gross, Cyril Chappellet, and Hall Hibbard. / *Lockheed California Company*

Left: Clarence L. 'Kelly' Johnson, father of the P-38 (and many advanced designs to follow), was discovered by Chief Engineer Hall Hibbard at the University of Michigan in 1933 when Johnson wrote a report critical of the Electra's initial tail design. / *Lockheed California Company*

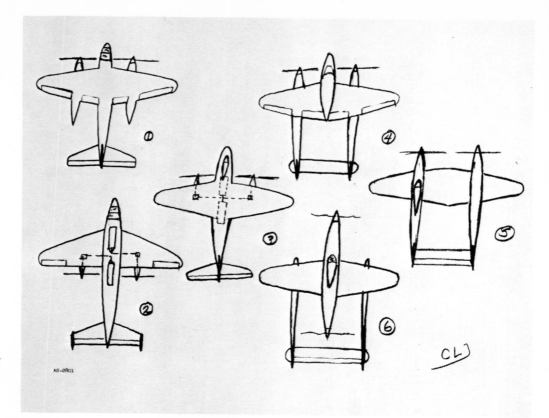

Right: Sketches of six designs roughed out by Kelly Johnson for the 1937 Air Corps fighter competition. Number four was selected.
/ Lockheed California Company

Below: Original patent drawing of the XP-38, filed 27 June 1939, lists Hall L. Hibbard and Clarence L. Johnson as inventors.
/ Lockheed Aircraft Corporation

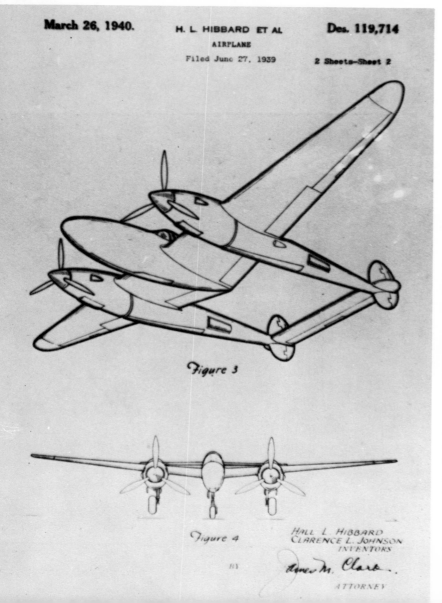

March 26, 1940. H. L. HIBBARD ET AL Des. 119,714
AIRPLANE
Filed June 27, 1939 2 Sheets-Sheet 2

Figure 3

Figure 4

HALL L. HIBBARD
CLARENCE L. JOHNSON
INVENTORS
BY
ATTORNEY

development of the Model 10 Electra, which first flew in February 1934, and it was Hibbard who first recognised the design genius of the man who would become Lockheed's most famous engineer, Clarence L. 'Kelly' Johnson.

Johnson was doing graduate work at the University of Michigan when a scale model of the Electra was sent there for wind tunnel tests early in 1933. When Johnson wrote a report critical of the Electra's tail assembly, Hibbard was impressed. He promptly hired Johnson; and thus laid the cornerstone for Lockheed's well known 'Skunk Works'.

Preliminary drawings of the Model 22 were prepared in a matter of days, starting with freehand sketches by Kelly Johnson. The Air Corps wanted a craft for the 'tactical mission of interception and attack of hostile aircraft at high altitudes.' Specifics included a true air speed of 360mph at altitude, and climb to 20,000ft within six minutes.

These figures imposed a power requirement that dictated the use of two engines, since no single engine of sufficient power then existed. Also inherent in the request was the obvious necessity of employing Allison liquid-cooled engines. The Air Corps had become convinced several years before that the high-horsepower liquid-cooled engine offered more possibilities with turbo supercharging at high altitudes than did the big air-cooled radials. Therefore, the Army had contributed development funds to Allison (a small subsidiary of General Motors

Corporation) for its V-1710 project as early as December 1932; and when the Lockheed Model 22 drawings were completed in February 1937, the Allison V-1710-C8 was just a few weeks away from its first successful test at 1,000hp. It was America's only big liquid-cooled engine near production status.

Lockheed President Robert Gross personally delivered the Model 22 drawings to Wright Field, Ohio, and, four months later, the Army indicated its approval of the design. Air Corps Contract 9974, dated 23 June 1937, authorised construction of one airplane. It would be designated XP-38, and assigned Air Corps serial number 37-457.

Construction of the XP-38 did not begin until 13 months later, and delivery to the Air Corps was made on New Year's Day 1939. Disassembled, it was loaded on three trucks, concealed by canvas, and taken from the Lockheed plant at Burbank to March Field, near Riverside, California.

Meanwhile, events had conspired to place Lockheed in a more favourable financial position. The Electra had been scaled-up to a 14-place midwing transport for which the Japan Air Line Company (Dai Nippon) placed a timely order. It was timely because these craft were coming down the production line when a British purchasing commission arrived in the US in April 1938, in search of airplanes to belatedly bolster Britain's defences in the face of Adolf Hitler's mounting aggressions. As Cyril Chappellet later told it, 'If we hadn't had this (Japanese) business, our factory would have been empty and the British would hardly have dared to place contracts with a concern that was not in production.'

Although Lockheed had but five days' notice to prepare for the British visit, a combination of long hours and frantic effort during that time produced a full-scale wooden mock-up of a Model 14 converted to a medium reconnaissance bomber. The British liked it; and the Air Ministry soon approved an order for 250 such machines, which they designated the Hudson, at a total cost of $25million. It was the largest single order ever received by any US aircraft builder. It allowed Lockheed to market $4.25million in stock, and begin an expansion programme that saw the company grow from 2,500 employees in January 1939, when the XP-38 was delivered, to 50,000 workers in January 1941, when the first YP-38 service test machine was delivered.

It would be yet another year before P-38 production reached 150 units per month; and although the Lightning entered combat quite early, F-4 versions went to Australia in April 1942 and P-38E models were sent to the Aleutians in June of that year, still another year would pass before this unique and deadly craft could honestly be called 'combat ready'. But that didn't matter. The enemy was upon us, and we were obliged to fight with what we had.

P-38 Development

Nine days after the XP-38 arrived at March Field, it was ready to fly; in the quiet, hazy chill of a Southern California winter morning, the man who would fly it stood for a time, silently looking at this ominously-beautiful craft. Lt Benjamin S. Kelsey was not a talkative man, but his thoughts would not be difficult to guess. The XP-38 represented a quantum advance in fighter aircraft design, and it surely possessed secrets, perhaps dangerous secrets.

Kelsey, however, was an experienced and highly proficient pilot. He had received his commission in the US Army Air Corps 10 years before (promotion in rank was agonisingly slow in the US Army during the twenties and thirties), and his record was such that it had earned him the job of XP-38 project officer.

The twin Allisons were grumbling impatiently, and at last Kelsey climbed aboard. The XP-38's cockpit was a familiar place, because he had spent countless hours there during construction and assembly of the big fighter.

It was indeed big for a fighter* airplane. Its wings spanned 52ft, and its weight exceeded 15,000lb. Its Allison V-1710-C9 engines, V-1710-11 and -15 Air Corps designations, were rated at 1,090hp at 13,200ft. The left one rotated clockwise (as viewed from the rear), and the right engine counter-clockwise, thus countering the effects of torque and the spiralling propeller wash.

Now, General (retired) Ben S. Kelsey picks up the story and recalls for us the significant events in the XP-38's short life:

'During the taxi tests, everything seemed to work well except the wheel brakes. We didn't have an airplane then that landed as fast as the XP-38, and of course it was necessary to establish that its brakes were adequate. On a high-speed taxi run, I ran out of runway after the wheels expanded with

Below: Boldly designed, the XP-38 reached beyond the knowledge of the best aerodynamicists. At right is a Douglas B-18 Bolo bomber. */ Lockheed Aircraft Company*

*The term 'interceptor', along with the manner in which XP-38 specifications were originally drawn, were largely dictated by the need to present it as a purely defensive weapon; the only kind the US Congress was likely to approve or pay for at the time.

heat and lost braking power. I went into a ditch, but didn't damage the airplane.

'We used a hand braking system finally, that was put together from a cylinder taken from a Northrop A-17, and an extra hydraulic oil tank. The idea behind the extra fluid was to allow the pilot to pump more oil into the system after he ran out of brakes. This enabled me to keep the pressure up, but if I used brakes, they would be gone after two normal landings. Therefore, the obvious technique with this prototype aircraft would be to land it without wheel brakes.

'This called for dragging-in low, in landing configuration, and using just enough power to hold the plane slightly above stall. Then, chop power as soon as the runway slid under the nose. This is what led to loss of the plane later at Mitchel Field; I'll return to that in a moment.

'On the first test flight, which was delayed until 27 January because of the braking problem, I had a Ford Trimotor as a chase plane, which may help put this in perspective timewise. Just after I lifted the wheels, the plane developed a very severe flutter, wing flutter. It wasn't mild; the amplitude of the flutter at the tip was of the order of two or three feet. There wasn't enough runway left to land on and, looking at the wing and wondering what to do, I saw a piece of the flap bouncing up, so I retracted the flaps; Lockheed you see, had said to use half-flaps for take-off. As the Fowler flaps came back into the wing, the flutter stopped.

'I landed without using the flaps, and when we made an inspection we found that three of the four aluminium flap-control link rods had broken, allowing the flaps to run out to the end of their travel and whip up over the trailing edge. These were replaced with steel link rods, which solved that problem.

'Later, we found that this flap arrangement was subject to buffeting in the take-off speed range at the half-flap setting, and also at the full-flap setting during landing approach at minimum speed. We soon discovered that this resulted from insufficient tolerance at the flaps' leading edge which was pinching-off the airflow. Kelly Johnson cut holes in the skin of the well the flaps went into and solved this on the YP models that followed. But, meanwhile, it meant we had to cut the engines to get the flaps down prior to landing. It was a bad way of doing things, but did allow us to go forward with the initial tests.

'These tests, during the next couple of weeks, which totalled about five hours' flying time, did establish that the plane handled well, and that its performance would easily fall within the parameters we had calculated. We had only minor problems. There was no trouble with the controls; rigging was excellent, and the engines performed well, except for some concern that the early turbo supercharger systems would not produce enough carburettor heat at low rpm to combat carburettor ice under some conditions.

Below: The XP-38 was powered with Allison V-1710-11/15 (C-9) engines rated at 1,090hp each at 13,200ft. It was easily capable of 400mph above 15,000ft. It was first flown 9 January 1939, with Lt Benjamin S. Kelsey at the controls. */ Lockheed Aircraft Corporation*

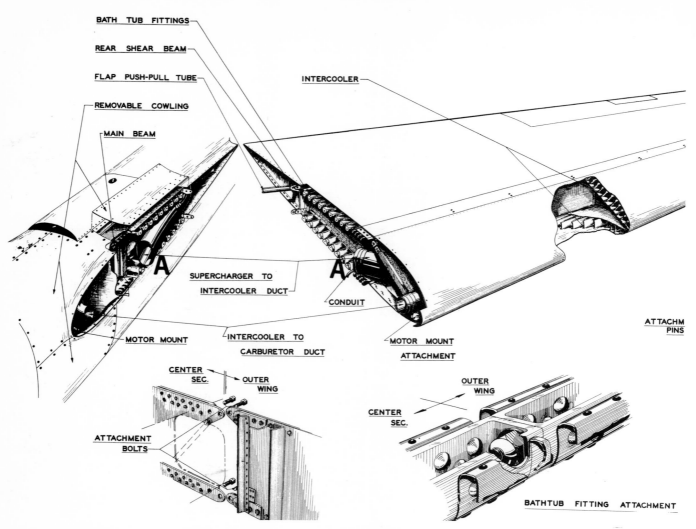

BATH TUB FITTINGS

REAR SHEAR BEAM

FLAP PUSH-PULL TUBE

REMOVABLE COWLING

MAIN BEAM

INTERCOOLER

SUPERCHARGER TO
INTERCOOLER DUCT

CONDUIT

MOTOR MOUNT

INTERCOOLER TO
CARBURETOR DUCT

MOTOR MOUNT
ATTACHMENT

ATTACHM
PINS

CENTER
SEC.

OUTER
WING

ATTACHMENT
BOLTS

OUTER
WING

CENTER
SEC.

BATHTUB FITTING ATTACHMENT

Above: Supercharger inter-coolers formed part of the wings' leading edges in early P-38s and were a continuing source of trouble.

'Now, there has been a lot of comment about us losing the XP-38 at Mitchel Field after a transcontinental flight; but the point was that General Arnold, Chief of Air Corps, was being very hard pressed in Washington about such things as record-breaking German airplanes, and the new British Spitfire... Since it was apparent that, when we delivered the XP-38 from March to Wright Field in Ohio, we'd be flying it at its normal cruising speed, substantially the same speed as Howard Hughes' cross-country record in a specially designed racer, we felt that this would give General Arnold some impressive figures to use in his appropriations battle with the Congress...

'I was ordered to deliver the plane to Wright Field on 11 February 1939... it was strictly a delivery flight at standard cruise... I landed at Amarillo 2hr 48min after leaving March Field. Another 2hr 45min put me down at Wright Field.

'When I climbed from the plane at Wright Field, there was a discussion concerning the time I had made, and it was noted that, with the time on the ground at both Amarillo and Dayton, there was no possibility of bettering

Hughes's record. But in terms of flying time, we could do considerably better because his had been a non-stop flight. It was just a question of whether we wanted to go to Mitchel and back, or call it a day with the planned delivery.

'Then, in his sort of brusque way, General Arnold said, "Go ahead, Kelsey. Take it."

'I averaged 360mph true air speed, and it was clear to me that the XP-38 would easily do 400mph if pressed. My flying time between March and Mitchel Fields was 7hr 2min.

'Descending into Mitchel, I think I probably picked up carburettor ice. This was a problem that had not been solved, and the early B-17s had the same trouble. There simply wasn't enough heat available via the superchargers at low rpm to handle carburettor ice. I had to throttle way back to lower the flaps; and then, since I was faced with a landing without wheel brakes, it was necessary to "drag it in" under power at low speed. But the flap problem and the brake problem were just waiting for one additional problem, lack of power at a critical time, to produce disaster. As I attempted to ease-in

14

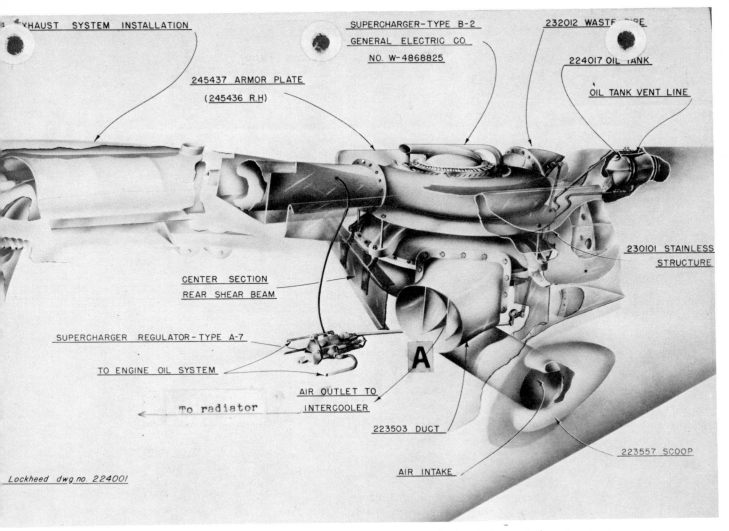

EXHAUST SYSTEM INSTALLATION

SUPERCHARGER-TYPE B-2
GENERAL ELECTRIC CO.
NO. W-4868825

232012 WASTE PIPE

224017 OIL TANK

OIL TANK VENT LINE

245437 ARMOR PLATE
(245436 R.H)

230101 STAINLESS
STRUCTURE

CENTER SECTION
REAR SHEAR BEAM

SUPERCHARGER REGULATOR-TYPE A-7

TO ENGINE OIL SYSTEM

A

To radiator

AIR OUTLET TO
INTERCOOLER

223503 DUCT

223557 SCOOP

AIR INTAKE

Lockheed dwg no. 224001

power, the engines failed to respond. Both continued to idle nicely; but wouldn't accelerate. I was low and slow on final approach. Without power, there was nothing I could do to add a single inch to that approach. I struck the ground short of the runway. The aircraft was a total loss; I was uninjured.

'Tom McRae and his crew from Allison listed nine possible causes for the engines' failure to accelerate. I had eliminated five of them prior to the crash, fuel selector switch, boost pumps, etc, and the four remaining possibilities were eliminated by re-design of the fuel and carburettor systems on the follow-on YP models...

'The next day, I was in Washington to explain why I'd busted our new airplane. General Arnold listened to my account, then took me around with him to the Secretary of War, and to the Bureau of the Budget; and I guess we went to four or five top level people. In each case, the General would say to me, "Kelsey, tell him about that new '38." So I'd tell each how fast it was, how nicely it handled, and so on.

'And within 60 days, that's 60 days mind you, Lockheed had a contract for service-test quantities of the YP-38. There's no way in the world that Lockheed could have received such a contract that soon, had the XP-38 remained in existence, because then it would have been necessary to validate all its performance estimates, write-in a lot of specifics, and probably wait while it was returned to the factory for modifications. Therefore, we significantly cut time between the X model and the Y models as a result of losing the first one. The same thing happened when we lost the first B-17 at Wright Field. It was tragic; but not having the prototype to nit-pick for a contract, which you must do, you simply go ahead with a design that has already demonstrated certain basic things before its loss.'

The order for 13 service-test YP-38s was Air Corps Contract 12523, dated 27 April 1939. However, the first YP-38 did not fly until 16 September 1940, and the last one was not delivered until eight months after that. During those critical 25 months, the 'course of human events' was altered for generations

Above: Turbo supercharger system, beginning with the P-38J models, moved inter-coolers beneath the engines (increasing internal fuel by 110gal). This improved supercharger efficiency, but sometimes allowed engine oil to over-cool if not properly monitored by the pilot.

Above: XP-38 is refuelled at Wright Field pending decision by General Arnold as to the feasibility of extending Kelsey's cross-country dash to Mitchel Field, New York.

Right: General Henry H. 'Hap' Arnold, Chief of Air Corps, orders Lt Kelsey to continue flight to Mitchel Field. / *Ben Kelsey*

to come. Still, another nine months would pass before Lockheed achieved anything resembling mass production of the P-38. Total production for 1941 would amount to 196 units (exclusive of the YPs), none of which were fit for combat. Meanwhile, desperate orders piled up. Britain ordered 667 P-38s in March 1940; and the US Army Air Corps* contracted for 673 five months later.

Although we may tend to fault Lockheed for taking so long to get the P-38 into meaningful production, any of us who are old enough to recall those fearful times, the confusions, the shortages, the frustrating urgency to do a thousand things at once to fill a thousand pressing needs, will be able to put this, and other 'failures' into proper perspective. Attempting to arm ourselves and defend our freedom, we demanded production miracles of our often poorly funded industries to make up for 20 years of complacency, incompetency, and wishful thinking on the part of our leaders.

*The US Army Air Corps became the US Army Air Forces on 20 June 1941.

Lockheed, as the rest of the US, British, and Commonwealth industry, did the best it could with what it had when there wasn't enough of anything, from metal to money to manpower, to go around; and did so according to assigned priorities. In addition to P-38s, Lockheed was building Venturas, Hudsons, and Boeing B-17s in large numbers. Meanwhile, the financing of plant expansion programmes in America had to depend upon private money sources until the US Congress at last enacted the Lend - Lease Bill (HR 1776) on 11 March 1941.

There were other factors that slowed P-38 development and production. The YP-38's internal structure was practically designed from scratch, because the XP-38 had been handbuilt by the 'cut and fit' method, and its airframe did not lend itself to efficient mass production techniques. The Army also demanded that the YP models be at least 1,500lb lighter than the experimental model. Finally, there were some important aerodynamic lessons to be learned, and a number of detail improvements to be made before the P-38's true potential could be

Below: First YP-38 made its maiden flight 16 September 1940, with Lockheed Chief Pilot Marshall Headle at the controls. Counter-rotating props turned outwards. Propeller cuffs were later removed. Note lack of wing-fuselage fillet. */ Lockheed Aircraft Corporation*

Right: The YP-38 was fitted with Allison V-1710-27/29 (F-2) engines rated at 1,150hp. Elevator mass balances were added later as a solution for tail buffeting at high speed. Wing fillets solved that, but the mass balances remained on all subsequent P-38s.
/ Lockheed Aircraft Corporation

Below: A YP-38 emerges from a cocoon of Hudsons at the Lockheed factory into an early spring morning in 1941.
/ Lockheed California Company

tapped. It all took time, and time was the most precious commodity of all.

The first YP-38 completed, s/n 39-689, was retained at the factory, although its USAAF record card reveals that it was flown but 23 hours during its 14 months of existence. Clearly, Lockheed left much of the YP-38 test flying to the Army pilots. Delivery of the remaining dozen YP-38s to the Army was completed in May 1941; and it was then that the spectre of compressibility first showed iteslf.

Major Signa A. Gilkie experienced it first. He took YP-38 s/n 39-694 well above 30,000ft then entered a dive. As the airspeed needle swung past 320mph, somewhere around 500mph true air speed at that altitude, the airplane's tail began to buffet severely. Then, as the dive continued, the craft became progressively nose-heavy, increasing its dive angle to near vertical, while the control yoke oscillated stiffly and defied Gilkie's utmost efforts to pull it back and effect recovery. Unwilling to bail out and lose the plane to this strange and frightening force, the major tried the only small remedy left to him. He cranked-in 'nose-up' elevator trim.

At first, the elevator trim tab seemed ineffective; but as the plane entered denser air below 18,000ft, the nose began to swing upward. Full control quickly returned, and seconds later, Major Gilkie found himself straight and level at 7,000ft.

He had also found the two major aerodynamic problems that represented the price Lockheed must pay for pioneering with

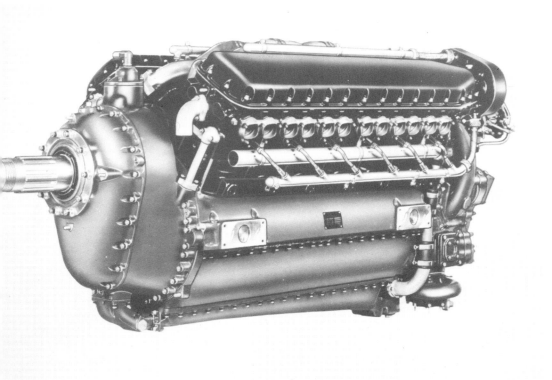

Left: The Allison V-1710 F-series engine which powered the YP-38s and all production models of the Lightning was rated at 1,150hp in the YPs; 1,325hp in the P-38s, and was up to 1,425hp (1,600hp war emergency) in the P-38J models. / *Allison Division, GM*

Below: Dr Sanford A. Moss, America's supercharger pioneer (right), with Brig-Gen James H. Doolittle and the General Electric Type B turbo supercharger which was fitted to engines in the 800-1,400hp range. / *General Electric Company*

a high-speed high-altitude fighter. He had encountered in quick succession, a dangerous tail buffeting, followed by aerodynamic compressibility.

It took a while to figure out that the two problems were not related. Most Lockheed engineers believed that there was but one problem, an improperly balanced tail. This resulted in the installation of external mass balance weights on the elevator (which remained on all subsequent P-38s, although Kelly Johnson has always maintained that they were useless). Other 'fixes' were applied, including strengthening of the horizontal stabiliser and increased tension of the elevator control cables; but the cause of the tail flutter was isolated a month later by wind tunnel tests at Cal Tech which showed that there had been nothing wrong with the tail in the first place. Under certain extreme conditions, it was simply being buffeted by a

strongly turbulent airflow created at the sharp junctures where wing and fuselage were joined. About 40 wing fillet shapes were tried until one was found that properly smoothed-out the airflow over the tail in all flight regimes.

Although the tail flutter problem was thus rather quickly eliminated, the little understood phenomenon of compressibility remained. Late that summer, flying the first YP-38, Lockheed test pilots Jimmy Mattern, Ralph Virden and Milo Burcham cautiously began nibbling at high-altitude dives, limiting themselves to an indicated air speed of 295mph above 30,000ft. Then, on 4 November, Virden took this airplane aloft for a series of dives, working upward from 15,000ft. The 'number one' YP-38, which had by then accumulated slightly over 23 hours' flight time, had been fitted with new spring loaded servo tabs on the elevator's

Below: Instrument panel of the P-38G-15.

Above: The 1st Pursuit Group received the first production P-38s in mid-1941. Only 29 of the first model were built. / *USAF*

Left: Built concurrently with first production P-38s, though not delivered to the Air Corps until a year later, was the pressurised XP-38A. It was not developed. / *Lockheed California Company*

Below left: The Lockheed XP-49 was another pressurised version of the P-38, powered with experimental Continental XIV-1430 inverted engines of 1,350hp. It was Lockheed Model 522; s/n 40-3055. / *Mitch Mayborn*

Above: One of 36 P-38Ds built takes-off from Burbank, September 1941.
/ *American Aviation Historical Society*

Right: The P-38E contained many detail changes, plus a switch to the 20mm cannon in place of a 37mm; Curtiss electric props, new internal operating systems, and nose-wheel retract-arm moved behind nose-wheel strut. Some Es saw combat in the Aleutians and, as F-4s, in New Guinea.
/ *American Aviation Historical Society*

Bottom right: Another of the original 29 production machines, s/n 40-744, had superchargers removed and an extra cockpit installed in port boom as an experimental trainer. / *USAF*

22

trailing edge (company sources today don't agree as to whether there was one or two such tabs) which, acting opposite to elevator deflection when the control yoke force reached 30lbs would substantially add to the pilot's muscle in elevator control: in other words, elevator boost aerodynamically induced.

Virden successfully completed the lower altitude dives, reaching true air speeds of up to 535mph; but it is not known just how high he went to begin his final dive. What is known is that the new tabs apparently worked so well that Virden pulled the tail off the airplane at about 3,000ft in a dive recovery, and died in the ensuing crash.

The loss of this airplane and pilot established little, except that the P-38 wasn't going to be 'muscled out' of its compressibility problem.

Meanwhile, a total of 68 planes had been built, not counting the XP and YP models: 29 P-38s, 36 P-38Ds, and three P-38Es. Delivery of the production models had begun in June and by the end of October 1941, delivery of the P-38Es had started.

Only 210 P-38Es were built during the next five months, then the P-38F entered production in April 1942. But it was not until P-38Gs were coming off the production line in October 1942, that a P-38 scale model was at last accepted for high-speed wind tunnel tests at NACA's Ames Laboratory. This was, perhaps, the single most significant lapse in P-38 development. Since Maj Gilkie's dive had first revealed the seriousness of the problem, 17 irretrievable months had slipped by.

However, once the engineers could watch the shock waves form on the P-38 wing at Mach .67, giving them visible evidence of its effect on the airplane, the problem was at least positively defined, if not solved. They discovered that air passing over the curved parts of the model increased in velocity by as much as 40 per cent. This meant that the airflow over the wing (this particular wing) could reach the speed of sound when the airplane's true air speed was but 67 per cent of the speed of sound; and the shock wave which then followed rendered the airplane uncontrollable.

Actually, several things could be done to raise the P-38s critical Mach number (the Spitfire hit compressibility at Mach .83, primarily because of its very thin wing). A new wing would do it; and a stretched pilot's nacelle would also help. But at the end of 1942, with production of the P-38G at last approaching 150 units per month, and the USAAF desperate for more, major design

Below: Lockheed 'Swordfish' was a greatly modified P-38E, s/n 41-2048, used for in-flight research of laminar-flow airfoils and the study of boundary layer air control. */ Mitch Mayborn*

Left: P-38E, s/n 41-1986, was given up-swept tail as a possible remedy for high-speed tail buffeting. 'High-tailing it' wasn't the answer; wing fillets solved the problem. / *Lockheed California Company*

Right: Lockheed XP-58 *Chain Lightning* had span of 70ft, and was powered with a pair of 3,000hp Allison V-3420 engines (an X-configured engine resulting from the mating of two V-1710s), and armament was planned as two remotely-controlled turrets, each mounting a pair of .5in guns, plus four 37mm cannons in the nose. It first flew 6 June 1944. / *Mitch Mayborn*

Below: The P-38H-5s were the first to have the bar added to the national insignia. / *USAF*

changes, with the attendant re-tooling, testing, etc, were out of the question. America was fighting for her life, and no time remained to exploit this hard won knowledge with the P-38. Production was all-important.

This urgent need, however, did not preclude a modification of another kind. If they couldn't push back compressibility, Lockheed engineers decided, they could at least stay out of it. Therefore, a dive brake was devised; one that could be 'bolted on' to the airframe without slowing production. This modification took the form of a pair of accordian-type flaps attached to the main wing beam (spar), and positioned just beyond each engine boom, 30 per cent of the chord behind the wing's leading edge. When not in use these flaps retracted flush into the bottom of the wing. They were electrically activated by means of a trigger on the control wheel.

The dive brakes were effective. It was still possible to find compressibility at dive angles exceeding 60 degrees from very high altitudes; but despite buffeting, and the danger of exceeding the airplane's structural design limits, control remained.

Although dive brakes were installed on a test machine in late February 1943, and Ben Kelsey (by then a colonel) flew the craft and approved the devices early in April, Lockheed was unable to incorporate this important modification into P-38 assembly lines for another 14 months. By that time, 5,300 P-38s had been built, more than half of the ultimate total.

In a taped interview, General Kelsey told us that the dive brakes on the test airplane were hydraulically controlled, and this system failed on his final dive test. He entered compressibility, and pulled the tail off the airplane attempting recovery. Kelsery bailed out, sustaining a broken ankle. The General described in detail the hydraulic system malfunction. There was no seat cushion involved as had been previously reported. On production aircraft, the dive brakes were electrically activated.

The dive brake modification appeared on the last 210 J models, the P-38J-25s, produced

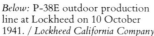

Below: P-38E outdoor production line at Lockheed on 10 October 1941. / *Lockheed California Company*

in June 1944. By that time, other important improvements had accrued, hydraulic aileron boost, better cockpit heating, a flat, bullet-proof windscreen, manoeuvring flaps (a control which allowed a quick, eight-degree extension of the Fowler flaps), an adequate inter-cooler system, and improved engines with supercharging automatically controlled; *that* was when one could say that the P-38 Lightning was ready to fulfil its long-awaited promise; that was when it could be accurately described as a long-legged, high-altitude combat aircraft of truly fearsome proportions, that gave up nothing to any enemy aircraft anywhere in any flight regime. The potential had been there all the while. Had it been exploited, say, two years earlier, a reasonable hope, since in fact the P-38 required seven years to mature, this rugged and versatile fighter (with a bomb capacity equalling that of the B-25 Mitchell) may indeed have greatly altered the course of World War II. However, there is ample evidence that the P-38 provided the means for a substantial altering of that conflict, as it was.

Above: The H and J model Lightnings used the same engines, V-1710-89/91 (Allison F-15 series). Flat, bullet-proof windscreen appeared on the P-38J-10 (above). / *Lockheed Aircraft Corporation*

Right: Factory-fresh P-38J-15 during its production test flight. A total of 1,400 J-15s were built, and 350 J-20s followed before the J-25 model at last appeared with dive brakes and aileron boost. / *Edward Jablonski*

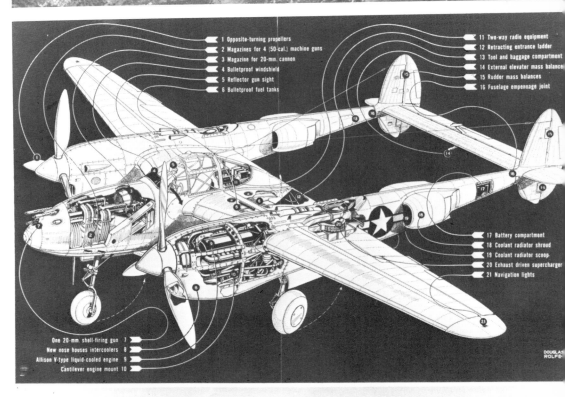

1 Opposite-turning propellers
2 Magazines for 4 (50-cal.) machine guns
3 Magazine for 20-mm. cannon
4 Bulletproof windshield
5 Reflector gun sight
6 Bulletproof fuel tanks

11 Two-way radio equipment
12 Retracting entrance ladder
13 Tool and baggage compartment
14 External elevator mass balance
15 Rudder mass balances
16 Fuselage empennage joint

17 Battery compartment
18 Coolant radiator shroud
19 Coolant radiator scoop
20 Exhaust driven supercharger
21 Navigation lights

One 20-mm. shell-firing gun 7
New nose houses intercoolers 8
Allison V-type liquid-cooled engine 9
Cantilever engine mount 10

DOUGLAS ROLFE

LOCKHEED P-38 LIGHTNING

Lockheed P-38 Lightning has wing span of 52 feet, length of 37 feet, 10 inches, and over all height of 11 feet, 6 inches. Speed is "well over 400 mph" and she will climb to an altitude of

Aleutians and North Atlantic Ferry

Lockheed model 322 was built for
the RAF which called it the
Lightning MkI. It lacked
superchargers and counter-rotating
props. The RAF rejected it, and the
USAAF re-engined 138 Lightning
Is and used them for training.
/ Mitch Mayborn

Above: The P-38F-1 appeared in April 1942, and featured new pylon racks beneath the centre wing section designed to carry a ton of external ordnance. Maximum speed was 395mph at 25,000ft with a combat weight of 15,900lb. Service ceiling was 39,000ft.
/ *Mitch Mayborn*

Right: A P-38F-5 with a Spitfire MkII reveals difference in size. The 'Spit' possessed but forty per cent of the P-38s weight, but lacked the Lightning's great versatility.
/ *Merle Olmsted Collection*

Bottom right: Recon photo reveals a dozen Japanese 'Rufes' (Nakajima A6M2-N floatplane fighter) in Kiska Harbor. / *USAF*

We shall probably never know all the facts attendant to Britain's order for 667 P-38s, approved by the Air Ministry in March 1940. The first 143 of these craft, designated Lightning MkIs, were so clearly unfit for combat that one wonders if Lockheed had to grit its corporate teeth and look the other way while building them. More to the point, is the question of why Britain should place such an order, because the Lightning I was without effective armour, had no superchargers, and its early model Allisons of 1,090hp rotated in the same direction. Thus robbed of its primary design function, that of high-altitude fighter, the big and relatively heavy Lightning could hardly promise performance advantages over aircraft the RAF already possessed. The balance of the order, for P-38F-13, -15, and G-15 models, seemed more plausible, although those machines were not scheduled for delivery until mid 1943.

Therefore why, two months before France fell, and four months before the Battle of Britain, did the Air Ministry approve a large order (actually totalling more airplanes than all the Spitfires and Hurricanes then possessed by Fighter Command) for an untested American fighter due for delivery up to three years later? Perhaps it was a prudent just-in-case-we-need-it act. But it is at least possible that it represented a modicum of collusion between General Arnold and his friends in the Air Ministry.

Suppose that General Arnold, desperate to circumvent the myopic US Congress and get combat aircraft production moving in the US, had said to the proper British authorities, 'Look here, fellows' (or words to that effect), 'we've got a 2,000hp fighter of great potential, but the program is barely alive. So far, I've been able to get money for only 65 of them. Somehow, I've got to get a real production line going and develop this airplane; it could prove very important to both of us a bit further down the turnpike. Now, if you will step in and place a large order for this craft immediately, that will set the program moving. Then, I'll promise to take you off the hook when the airplanes are ready for delivery if you don't want them.'

True, it is only a latter-day theory. But it could have happened that way. General Arnold cut a good many corners in an attempt to build US airpower, and we know that he employed a deception or two in his campaign to get the B-17.

Whether or not the British order actually cut P-38 development time and allowed Lockheed to achieve mass production sooner

Below: The 54th Fighter Squadron, equipped with P-38Es, was based at Adak in the Aleutians early in 1943. / *USAF*

Right: The face of the enemy; Japanese Naval airmen from film captured at Attu. / *USAF*

Below: Capt George Laven (right), and Lt Stanley Lang of the 54th FS. Laven was one of two P-38 pilots to fly the first fighter strike against Kiska on 3 September 1942, and later fought in the SW Pacific. / *USAF*

Far right, top: Capt Morgan Giffin briefs 54th FS pilots prior to a fighter sweep over the Aleutians. / *USAF*

Far right, bottom: Lightning F-5s in foreground have done their job and now stay at home while P-38s accompany Liberators on a raid to Attu. / *USAF*

than would have otherwise been possible, is difficult to determine. On paper, at least, the British order accelerated the P-38 programme by five months, because it was not until August 1940 that the USAAF at last ordered in quantity, signing a contract for 673 machines.

In any case, only a handful of Lightning MkIs was delivered to the RAF. British pilots flew three of them in a test programme, beginning in April 1942, but returned them to American hands as soon as they decently could, saying that the RAF would muddle along without the Lightning.

The Lightning MkIs still in America, apparently 138 of them, were accepted by the USAAF, sent to the Dallas Modification Centre for new engines, then went to Arizona as trainers. The P-38F-13s and -15s, and P-38G-15s (Lightning MkIIs), 524 machines in all, were also accepted by the USAAF and went to US fighter groups.

The name 'Lightning', bestowed upon the P-38s by the British in March 1940, was adopted by Lockheed, and the Lightning it was ever after.

Concurrent with production of the P-322s was the P-38E. The E model was fitted with Allison V-1710-27 and -29 engines of 1,150hp (sea level at 3,000rpm) which rotated outward from the pilot's nacelle. It had improved radios, a low pressure oxygen system, and a number of other detail improvements over the D model, and though it was not regarded as a combat-ready fighter, it did see action in the Aleutians, where the principal enemy was the weather.

Early in June 1942 the Japanese landed more than 3,000 soldiers on the Aleutian Islands of Attu and Kiska in a diversionary thrust primarily designed to lure the weakened US Navy into a showdown battle in the North Pacific. Admiral Nimitz refused to take the bait, however, and instead dry-gulched the vastly superior Japanese main force north of Midway, so grievously damaging the Japanese Navy that it never recovered. However, the Japanese presence in the Aleutians posed a threat (albeit of unknown dimensions) to Alaska and the North American Continent. The enemy could not be allowed to remain there. Therefore, a squadron of P-38s was hastily put together to join the 11th and 18th Fighter Squadrons (FS)* of the 28th Composite Group which had been in Alaska since the preceding December, when the Japanese attack on Pearl Harbor thrust the United States into World War II. The 11th and 18th were equipped with P-40s and P-39s, neither of which possessed sufficient range to carry the fight to the Nipponese at the extreme end of the 1,200 mile Aleutian Archipelago.

The P-40s had seen action when Japanese carrier-based aircraft attacked the US Naval

*In May 1942, all US pursuit groups were re-designated 'fighter groups', and the pursuit squadrons became 'fighter squadrons.' Normally, three fighter squadrons comprised a fighter group.

34

base at Dutch Harbor. Flying from a primitive airstrip at Otter Point on Umnak Island, 80 miles west of Dutch Harbor in the Eastern Aleutians, the P-40s shot down two 'Nates' (Nakajima Ki-43, Type 97) in an air battle there during the Attu and Kiska landings on 7 June.

Throughout the summer, however, the Japanese had appeared content to dig-in on Kiska, some 850 miles to the west of Umnak, and on Attu, 225 miles beyond Kiska, and forego further offensive action.

A first-hand account of P-38 operations in the Aleutians is provided to us by Col (ret) George Laven, now a sales and contract officer for McDonnell Douglas:
'I was in the 54th FS, which was sent from McChord Field, Washington, to Anchorage, Alaska, in the summer of 1942. The 54th had moved to Cold Bay, on the tip of the Alaskan Peninsula, when I arrived with two other P-38 pilots.

'Our first offensive mission came on 3 September, when Lt Victor E. Walton and I volunteered to hit Kiska from our strip on Umnak Island. On paper, it wasn't possible, and four other P-38 pilots who also volunteered had to turn back due to lack of fuel. Our P-38Es had 230 gallons (US) of internal fuel, and a normal consumption of 59 gallons per hour at 75 per cent power and 25,000ft. But Walton and I extended our range by holding high manifold pressure with low rpm settings, a cruise-control method

later taught to US pilots in the Pacific by Charles Lindbergh.

'We also believed that we had invented skip-bombing with our P-38s, but were later told that P-40 pilots had employed this tactic months earlier in the Philippines.

'We went after Japanese shipping at ten feet. On that first mission, I chose as a target a 10,000-ton Japanese freighter in Kiska Harbor; but our bomb fuses were often bad in those days, and my bomb went right through the ship without exploding. Walton and I approached Kiska from the northwest, screened by the 1,200ft ridges along that coast, at 14.32hrs. I crossed under Walton as we dropped down to the harbour to shoot-up a four engine Kawasaki Ki-97 flying boat, and then banked sharply left again to strafe the anti-aircraft guns which were thick along the north rim of the harbour. I then cut across the mouth of the harbour and left the area, heading out to sea in a southeasterly direction. Walton made a 180-degree turn over the docks on the harbour's south rim, hit a transport ship in the centre of the harbour, and went out the way we came in. We had both 20mm and .50-calibre ammunition remaining, but felt that fuel was too critical to warrant more passes. We made it back to Umnak with a few gallons to spare.

'All but 10 of the original 31 P-38 pilots in the Aleutians were killed there, most of them lost to the weather. In one case, four of us were flying the wing of a B-17 to a strip we

Above: Lt Herbert Hasenfus rode a pair of tiger sharks into combat over the Aleutians. / *Francis J. Pope*

Top left: When it wasn't ice and fog, it was rain and fog in the Aleutians. / *Mitch Mayborn*

Centre left: Lt Richard Bracey had 35 hours in P-38s when he went to the Aleutians, but logged 250 hours in the world's worst flying weather. All but 10 of the original 31 pilots of the 54th FS were killed in the Aleutians. / *Richard Bracey*

Bottom left: The .50 calibre guns normally carried 300 rounds of ammunition each; the 20mm cannon was fed by a 150-round drum. / *USAF*

had opened at Adak, about 375 miles west of Umnak. We were a very few feet off the water, and the fog was so bad that the number one man could not see numbers three and four of his formation. When we got to Adak, three and four were gone, they had hit a rock sticking out of the water. You can guess how close numbers one and two came to it. A number of P-38 pilots shot down in the water were alive when they hit; but we almost never recovered one alive. The frigid water killed them within minutes.

'In the fall of 1942, since we were not getting replacement aircraft, damaged but flyable P-38s were to fly back to the US for repairs or replacement. Four of us left Amchitka, where our people had built an airstrip only 75 miles from Kiska, and I was the only one who made it. We all got as far as Annette Island, but en route from there to Paine Field at Everett, Washington, we hit fog and two of our companions were never heard from again. The third got to Paine, but his hydraulic system was out, and by the time he got his wheels pumped down the field had socked-in. He landed long; skidded off the end of the runway. He survived, but the airplane didn't. I landed on Vancouver Island, which I found quite by chance. I then flew on to San Antonio where my plane was to be repaired; I had no flaps, having had them shot out. When my plane was fixed, I returned to Anchorage alone, then down the island chain to Amchitka on the wing of a B-24.

'The P-38 was the only airplane for that place, and also for the Southwest Pacific, because of its twin engines over water. Having two fans instead of one made a world of difference. The machine I flew in the

Left: The enemy also suffered from the Aleutian weather. Reconnaissance photo shows four floatplanes blown ashore and damaged by high winds at Attu. / *USAF*

Below: Capt Frank Shearin (left) and Lt John Geddes of the 54th FS with P-38H-5 at Adak, September 1943. / *Col (ret) Frank Shearin*

Aleutians was Serial Number 41-2076. Years larer, my own F-100 that I had when I commanded George Air Force Base, had the same last four numbers.'

The American base on Adak, and later on Amchitka, allowed US pilots to strike the enemy as often as weather permitted. A maximum effort strike on Kiska on 14 September 1942 consisted of 12 B-24s, 14 P-38s, and 14 P-39s. Two P-38s were lost when they collided over the target area. These were piloted by Lt Crowe and Major Jackson, the squadron's first commanding officer.

Lt-Col (ret) Richard Bracey, who now owns a lumber mill in Thomasville, Georgia, was another 54th pilot:

'I went directly from flying school to a P-38 training group at Paine Field in August 1942. I had 35 hours in P-38s when I was sent to the Aleutians that November. There, I logged about 250 hours, mostly in fog. I tangled with "Rufe" type "Zeros" (Nakajima A6M2-N Type 2, Model 12 fighter floatplane), weather, and flak . . .

'The best thing I remember about the P-38 is that it brought me home single-engine three times. It had a low stalling speed, no torque, and five fixed guns straight ahead. I flew the P-51 and it was a fine airplane; but give me a '38 anytime.'

Top: Ski-equipped P-38F and P-38J-1 (above) were tested in Alaska by Lt Randy Acord, but skis were not adopted for general use. / *American Aviation Historical Society*

Above: Most Lightnings in the Aleutians were lost to weather-related accidents. These are salvaged P-38L-5s at Shemya late in the war. / *USAF*

Left: Lightning F-5B-1 (P-38G-10) at Meeks Field, Iceland, 9 August 1943. Chalked notes on prop blades read: 'Oil 10qts, gas 535gal' / *USAF*

In September 1942 the three fighter squadrons in the Aleutians, 54th, 11th, and 18th, were formed into the 343rd Fighter Group of the 11th Air Force. At that time, RCAF fighter squadrons in Alaska, No 14 and 111, flying P-40 Kittyhawks, returned to Canada.

Throughout the winter and early spring (though it is hard to tell the difference in the Aleutians) the American fighters flew bombing and strafing missions to Attu and Kiska. Then on 11 May 1943 a US Navy task force put ashore on Attu the US Army's Seventh Division, and after fighting for nearly three weeks among the icy, fog-shrouded crags, the Seventh overwhelmed the 2,300 Japanese there, aided, as weather permitted, by the 11th Air Force.

Col (ret) Frank Shearin Jr, now executive vice president of the Happy Bear Corp, joined the 54th FS at Adak in December 1942, moving up to Amchitka when that strip was completed in March 1943:

'During the fighting on Attu, we tried to keep eight P-38s over the target during daylight hours. We carried one 500 or 1,000lb bomb, and one 165gal external fuel tank. On 24 May Group Commander Lt-Col Watt was shot down while attacking a formation of "Bettys" (Mitsubishi G4M1, Type 1 twin-engined attack/bomber). Only three of a flight of 25 "Bettys" returned home. John Gettes was also shot down, but was picked up uninjured by a Navy destroyer.

'We had two rules for dog-fighting the "Zeros" (Mitsubishi A6M1-8, Type 0, carrier-based fighter, Hamp/Zeke). Keep speed minimum of 300mph and always break hard-right and up. The Japanese fighters were over-powered for their airframes, and torque did not permit a tight, high-speed right turn.

'Speaking of performance, I returned to the United States in September 1943, and while in the pilots' lounge at Santa Maria Air Base, California, I overheard three P-38 student pilots scorning this airplane. They were saying the P-38 would not operate above 25,000ft, or if it would, their instructor would not take them. I found out their instructor's name and cleared a flight with the students.

'My briefing was short and to the point: "We're going to take this four ship formation up and we will continue to climb until one of you say 'Uncle.'" With that we took off. At 42,800ft indicating on the altimeter, I heard a garbled "uncle" being transmitted by a throat mike. 100 per cent oxygen under pressure made it difficult to speak at high altitude. The formation was climbing at 500ft per minute when the climb was terminated. That flight convinced them that the P-38 was a high-altitude aircraft.

'I later flew P-51s for about 250 hours. I rate the P-38 as the best overall fighter.'

Two months after Attu was recaptured, American troops invaded Kiska, only to

Below: The Japanese sent hundreds of incendiary devices across the North Pacific by free balloon during World War II in an attempt to start forest fires in Western Canada and the US Northwest. P-38s shot down this one over the ocean. / *USAF*

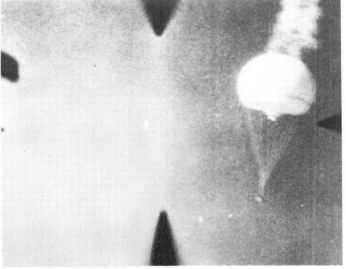
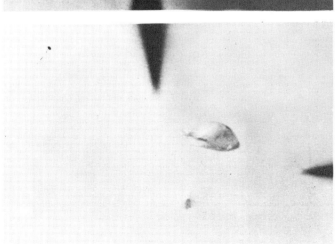
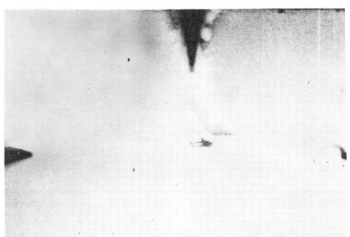

discover that the enemy had slipped away in the fog.

In October 1943 the 54th FS moved westward to the Island of Shemya to stand guard. The 11th and 18th, based at Adak, were to eventually receive P-38Ls in July 1945, and moved on to Shemya at that time.

Earlier, in the summer of 1942, at about the time the 54th FS arrived at Alaska, other P-38s were flying the North Atlantic to England.

British and Canadian pilots had been flying American-built multi-engined aircraft across the North Atlantic since 1939; but the ferrying of planes with lesser range demanded stepping-stone airstrips on Greenland and Iceland. A base on Iceland was prepared months before America was forced into the war. US Marines, supported by the P-40-equipped 33rd Pursuit Squadron of the 8th Pursuit Group, were sent there by President Roosevelt in July 1941 (The P-40s were flown off the deck of the Carrier *Wasp*). By mid-summer 1942, airstrips in Greenland, Bluie West One and Bluie West Eight, possessed radio navigational aids, and the build-up of US airpower in England began under the code name Operation Bolero.

During the rest of that year, a total of 882 aircraft out of 950 which started, most of them flown by young Americans who had never seen an ocean before, arrived safely. These included 366 heavy bombers, 150 medium bombers, 183 transports, and 178 P-38 Lightnings.

The Lightnings, P-38Fs and P-38F-1s, belonged to the 1st and 14th Fighter Groups, and were sheperded across, in flights of four, by B-17s of the 97th Bomb Group.

On 27 June 1942 80 Lightnings of the 94th, 27th, and 71st FSs, 1st FG, left Bangor, Maine, following 20 B-17Es of the 341st BS, 97th BG. All but two of the five-plane flights (four fighters, one bomber) completed the crossing without remarkable incident. Those two were Tomcat Yellow Flight, consisting of the B-17E *Dodo* and three P-38s; and Tomcat Green Flight led by B-17E *Big Stoop*, also with three P-38s. One P-38 had aborted from each flight at Bluie West One with mechanical problems.

The two drop-outs were fortunate, because the B-17s led the fighters into increasingly bad weather while BW-1 behind them at Narsasuak, Greenland became socked-in. Learning that their destination in Iceland was also closed, they tried BW-8 on Greenland's east coast only to find it, too, zero-zero.

Left: An operational loss, P-38F-5 s/n 42-12595, 50th FS, Iceland, 3 February 1944. / *USAF*

Below: P-38F-1s of the 27th FS, 1st FG, arrived in Iceland 6 July 1942, continued to England 28 August. / *USAF*

Right: 2-Lts Harry Stengle and James McNulty of the 50th FS shared a Ju88 over Iceland on 24 April 1943. / *USAF*

Below: During 1942, 178 Lightnings were flown to England via the North Atlantic ferry route, while 656 reached Britain by sea. / *USAF*

Finally, low on fuel, the two flights turned south to look for a place to land on the ice cap. With their choices limited, they were forced to accept a spot veined with crevasses. The first P-38 to go in lost its landing gear in a wheels-down landing, so the remaining Lightnings, and then the Fortresses, all landed wheel-up. Not one of the 25 men in the eight aircraft was seriously injured.

They were found within a couple of days by a B-24 Liberator piloted by Lt J. B. Long, and eventually rescued by dog sled. A recent note from a researcher in California informs that the airplanes are there today, in 'excellent condition.' The official USAAF report on the incident gives the location as 65° 20′ N; 45° 20′ W.

So, the 94th FS lost six of its airplanes, but no pilots, crossing the North Atlantic. The 50th FS, 14th FG, was not as fortunate.

On 1 August 16 Lightnings of the 50th FS left Goose Bay, Labrador, led by four B-17s, and over Davis Strait a P-38 piloted by Lt Goodrich simply disappeared. No one saw him go, though all aircraft were in visual contact with one another above a 7,000ft overcast, and Goodrich made no distress call on his radio.

He could not have been gone very long when he was missed, and Lt J. W. Williams, commanding the lead B-17, handed over his P-38s to another Fortress and turned back for a search below the overcast. The sea was rough beneath the 600ft ceiling, and visibility poor. Williams gave up after 45 minutes, and resumed his course.

Lightnings of the 94th, 71st and Headquarters Squadrons of the 1st FG arrived in England between 9 July and 25 July. The 27th FS, which had reached Iceland on 6 July, remained there until 28 August, adding some muscle to the defence duties of the 33rds P-40s.

During this time, Lt Elza E. Shahan of the 27th shared with P-40 pilot J. K. Shaffer credit for the first German aircraft destroyed in the European Theatre of Operations (ETO) by the USAAF in World War II when they shot down an FW200 Kurier, a four-engined armed reconnaissance plane, off the Icelandic coast on 15 August.

The 48th and 49th FSs of the 14th FG reached England during the last two weeks in August, permanently leaving behind in Iceland the 50th FS, which relieved the 27th. This allowed the 27th FS to join its sister units of the 1st FG in England.

The 1st FG was based at Ibsley, and the 14th FG at Atcham, Shrewsbury. Both groups belonged to the US 8th Air Force, formed in January 1942 for the coming attack on Hitler's Europe. However, even as the

Below: Langford Lodge, near Belfast, was a large modification and repair facility operated by Lockheed and the 8th Service Command. P-38F-5s and F-15s are identifiable here. / *USAF*

Lightning groups set about preparing for combat over the Continent, the exigencies of war had decreed that they fight elsewhere.

On 8 July Prime Minister Churchill had sent a message to President Roosevelt urging that they proceed with the invasion of North Africa, an operation they had previously discussed. Since the two leaders had already determined that the invasion of Europe was not feasible before the spring of 1944, Roosevelt agreed (after a 10-day delay due to initial opposition from his top Army and Navy commanders, General Marshall and Admiral King), and Operation Torch was scheduled for sometime in the fall. This resulted in establishment of the US 12th Air Force in August 1942, which would necessarily claim the P-38 units available in England.

Meanwhile, the P-38 groups engaged in practice sweeps over the Channel with RAF squadrons, practiced gunnery, simulated attacks on bomber formations, received instruction from British operations and intelligence officers, and familiarised themselves with British radio procedures.

Two-plane elements of the 1st FG were scrambled a number of times to intercept reported enemy aircraft; but the pilots were never told whether these were practice drills or for real. No enemy aircraft were sighted. The 94th FS lost Lt Charles Oakley to an operational accident near Thirsk. During October, the 14th FG flew several bomber escort missions to the French Coast, but encountered no enemy aircraft.

Then, on 24 October, the groups were alerted for movement. Their destination was, of course, unknown to them. Four days later, the ground echelons boarded ships at Liverpool, and the aircraft were flown to Land's End on England's southernmost tip. From there, they would fly to Gibraltar on 8 November the day Operation Torch was scheduled to begin. Many would not return.

Above: Delivery of the P-38G began in September 1942. The G models were fitted with Allison F-10 series engines (V-1710-51/55) which produced an extra 100hp at 25,000ft. The last 200 P-38G-10s could carry 1,800lb on each underwing pylon. / *Edward Jablonski*

Left: Newly arrived Lightnings on Queen's Drive in Liverpool being towed to Liverpool Airdrome, 9 January 1943. / *USAF*

Right: The P-38H series, with Allison F-15 (V-1710-89/91) engines of 1,425hp each, also received new superchargers and automatic oil temp control. Maximum speed at 25,000ft was 402mph. / *USAF*

Above: A 48th FS P-38F *Mickey* flown by
'Doc' Watson at Gibraltar staging field for
Operation Torch. / *Roger Freeman*

North Africa

When Operation Torch was launched on 8 November 1942 with Allied landings in North-west Africa, British and Commonwealth forces had been fighting the Germans and Italians in a see-saw war in North-east Africa for more than two years. However, just five days earlier, General Bernard Montgomery's British 8th Army had broken out of its defensive position at El Alamein in Egypt, and was pursuing Field Marshal Erwin Rommel's Afrika Korps westward into Libya. Therefore, Torch provided the western jaw of a giant pincer, 1,700 miles across, within which enemy forces in North Africa could be destroyed.

The key to ultimate victory in North Africa would be the successful interdiction of the enemy's supply lines across the Mediterranean, and the key to *that* was Allied airpower.

General Montgomery, who understood the proper use of airpower, could press his advantage confident that Air Marshal Tedder's Desert Air Force (which included the newly-formed US 9th Air Force) controlled the air over North-east Africa.

However, General Dwight Eisenhower, in overall command of Torch, had yet to learn the proper use of tactical airpower. He soon had General Jimmy Doolittle's US 12th Air Force spread thinly over 600 miles of North-west Africa to serve, piecemeal, the presumed needs of his ground commanders. The two P-38 groups, particularly the 14th FG, would pay heavily for this wasteful concept.

Below: Lightnings of the 48th FS, 14th FG, arrived in Algeria on 11 November 1942, three days after the invasion of North Africa by Allied forces under Eisenhower. / *USAF*

Operation Torch proceeded according to plan during the first days (except for behind-the-scene political moves involving the puppet French leaders). Allied forces went ashore at several points around Oran, Algiers, and at Mehedia (Port Lyautey), Safi, and Fedhala around Casablanca in French Morocco.

There were some resistance from Vichy French forces, but in the main the French had little inclination to fight, and all threw down their arms by 11 November.

On that day, at 13.30hrs, the first Lightning mission flown from African soil was carried out by pilots of the 48th FS, 14th FG. The P-38 groups, the 1st and 14th, had flown from Land's End to Gibraltar on the day of the invasion, and the 48th's air echelon was on the field at Tafaraoui on the 11th. The 49th FS arrived on the 18th. The 1st FG could put a few P-38s in the air from North Africa on the 20th. By then, the ground support people had found their air echelons, and the pilots were no longer required to fuel and arm their own machines.

The 48th FS moved to Maison Blanche on the 16th, and, that night, the Luftwaffe bombed and strafed the field, the Germans, along with some Italian troops, having arrived at El Aouina Airfield near Tunis just one day after the invasion. The hangars at Maison Blanche were severely damaged, and 18 aircraft received major damage, including seven P-38s.

On 18 November, the 48th FS flew its first official combat mission after gathering 12 Lightnings from the ruin visited upon the squadron two nights before. This was an escort of 20 C-47s to Constantine.

On 20 November the Germans returned to Maison Blanche with 20 Ju87s and Ju88s, destroying an entire British photo-recce unit, four Spitfires (there were two US fighter groups in the 12th AF equipped with Spitfires, the 31st and 52nd), three Beaufighters, a B-17, and two P-38s. Fortunately, the 1st FG (still not combat-ready), had moved to Nouvion earlier that day. The 14th's two squadrons moved the next day.

The 14th's new home was Youks les Bains, about 10 miles east of Tabessa in North-east Algeria. The 4,500ft runway at Youks was in a tiny valley, with foothills rising to 4,000ft on each side, and with a deep wash at one end. It was a forward base, so forward in fact that the only possibility of supply was by way of the 60th Troop Carrier Group's C-47 'Gooney Birds.' Sharing Youks with the 14th was a squadron of Douglas DB-7 light bombers manned by recently liberated French airmen, and some British paratroopers. On 25 November the 94th FS of the 1st FG also came to Youks, while the 71st FS returned to Maison Blanche for bomber escort duty.

Meanwhile, on the 21st, six P-38s of the 48th FS tangled with the Luftwaffe for the first time while escorting 12 Fortresses to Tunis. Near the target four Me109s were spotted and a 25-minute running battle ensued. Lt Carl Williams got one Messerschmitt when it attempted to dive

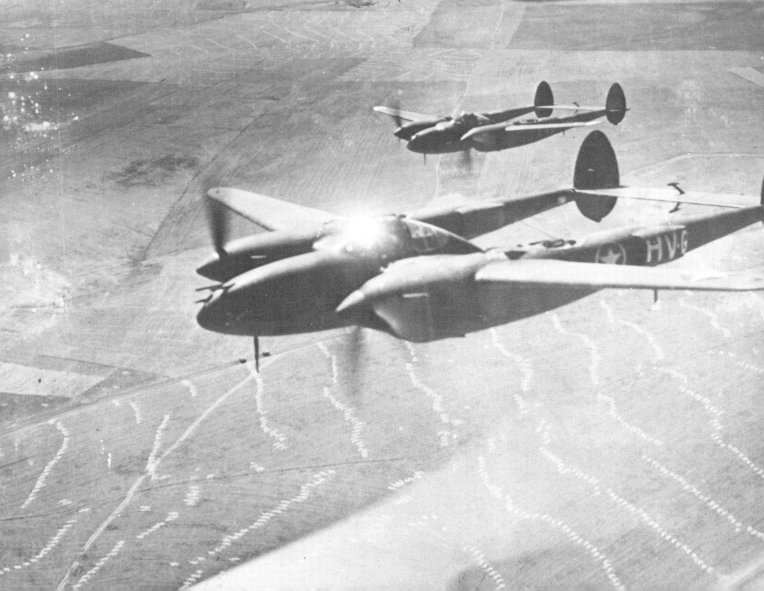

away from him. He quickly overtook the enemy and scored the first Lightning victory in Africa. Lt Ayers was injured when he was forced to crash-land due to battle damage.

The next day, pilots from both squadrons of the 14th FG flew a total of three missions and one intercept. To start the day properly, Capt Wade Walles, 48th FS CO, led five P-38s in a fighter sweep that accounted for a locomotive, four tanks, and . . . a motorcycle. The second mission of the day was for reconnaissance, but Lt Mark Shipham found an Italian twin-engine Breda which he sent crashing to earth. On the third mission Lts Sorensen and Tollen shot up a troop train, destroying its locomotive. Finally, Lts Sorensen and Shipman were standing alert at Youks late in the day when a Ju88 appeared over the field at about 9,000ft. They intercepted the enemy and scored hits on their first pass. One of Shipman's engines was hit, so he wheeled away, allowing Sorensen to follow the stricken bomber down until it crashed.

Three combat missions and an intercept in a day, that was to be the norm for the P-38s in North Africa. Throughout December 1942, one could count on a single hand the number of days the Lightnings failed to fly; and those were days of impossible flying weather. Or, perhaps more properly, those were the days when the big fighters simply could not be moved through the mud.

Mud was an enemy with which Allied planners had not reckoned. Expecting to make unopposed landings in Morocco and Algeria, and to grab the strategic town of Tunis in a quick thrust, British and American forces found themselves frustrated by the Germans' quick reaction, a great airlift of planes, tanks, and men from nearby Sicily, by lack of mobility when the rains came; and by committing their aircraft, a few at a time, to ground support missions and un-coordinated bombing raids, with no priority given to the defeat of German and Italian Air Forces and control of the air over North-west Africa.

The P-38s at Youks eventually triumphed over the mud. Lt Ervin Ethell's plane, *Tangerine*, was wrestled on to a smooth slope of solid rock that rose into the hills adjacent to the field. There was almost 1,700ft of it. Ethell taxied to the top, swung around and took-off downhill. He circled, then landed uphill. Youks was an all-weather field after all.

At least, it was for the airplanes. The men continued to live in the mud. Tents were the highest style of living until empty five-gallon cans were fashioned into an officer's club. Food was almost always K-Ration, except for some eggs and mutton bartered from local Arabs.

The mission assigned to the P-38s at Youks was that of air support for the Allied forces in Central Tunisia, which included the right flank of the US 1st Armored Division, and the British 78th Division. But this was air support as envisioned by local ground commanders.

Mission No 26 was typical, a reconnaissance to the Bizerte area flown by Lts Ethell and Skinner of the 48th FS, and Lts Butler and Evans of the 49th FS. Heading for El Arousa and anticipating heavy flak near Bizerte, the four Lightnings went down to the deck. Then, nosing over a hill by Lake Bizerte, they suddenly saw in the sky ahead a tight formation of 15 or 20 Ju52s, flying about 30ft above the water and escorted by four Me109s.

The P-38s fell upon the transports between Menzel and Metline. 'It was like flushing a covey of quail,' Ervin Ethell recalls. 'They tried to scatter, but we were on top of them.' Ethell methodically blasted four of the transports from the sky and was working on a fifth when he noticed that Skinner was in trouble with two Me109s. Ethell broke away from the Junkers, closed on the tail of one Messerschmitt and gave it a three-second burst with his cannon and four .50s. The German fighter went down behind a hill trailing smoke. But Skinner also went down.

Evans had accounted for a fifth Ju52. Then, separated and low on fuel, the three P-38s dived for the deck and headed home.

In addition to reconnaissance and ground attack assignments, the P-38s were much in

Above: The soft, often muddy wasteland at Youks took its toll. Berber tribesmen watch as salvage crew works. / *Kenneth M. Sumney*

Top left: Living conditions at Youks were on the primitive side; food was worse. Lightning in background has markings (HV-S) of 27th FS, stationed at Biskra. / *Kenneth M. Sumney*

Bottom left: Deluxe quarters at Youks shared by Lts Norman Jackson and John Caputo, the latter in entrance. Construction was dirt-filled five-gallon fuel tins. / *Norman W. Jackson*

demand for long-range bomber escort duty. Neither the 33rd FG's Warhawks, nor the 31st FG's Spitfires had the range of the Lightnings. Therefore, the P-38s were picked for the kind of missions that seemed to ensure a maximum of enemy opposition.

Meanwhile, the lack of replacement pilots and planes further eroded the Lightning groups' effectiveness. Most missions were flown with six to eight P-38s. Two and four-plane missions were not unusual; and 16 to 18 Lightnings for bomber escort (protecting 20 to 25 mediums or heavies) was a maximum effort.

Then, just before Christmas 1942, the Lightning-equipped 82nd FG (95th, 96th, and 97th FSs) arrived in North Africa, along with some replacement pilots for the 1st and 14th FGs. However, the 82nd was also under strength and, by the middle of January 1943, when Prime Minister Churchill and President Roosevelt met at Casablanca, the 1st, 14th, and 82nd FGs had a total of but 90 P-38s between them. Normally a single US fighter group would have 10 to 20 more airplanes than that.

Things could have been worse, had not the 3rd Photographic Reconnaissance Group landed its F-4 Lightnings at La Senia, Algeria a month earlier to take over one of the tough jobs the fighters had been trying to handle. The 3rd PhG, by the way, was commanded by the President's son, Col Elliot Roosevelt.

It is hardly possible to say too much in favour of the unarmed F-4/F-5 groups. Their s was a unique mission, composed of approximately equal parts of boredom and danger. And despite the fact that they

received little glory, no Lightning group contributed more to ultimate victory, in Africa and elsewhere. Since they almost always flew alone, their comrades seldom knew the cause when one failed to return.

During this period Lt Virgil Smith, the theatre's first American ace (48th FS), was himself shot down by an Me109 while on a bomber escort mission to Gabes. Two of his squadron mates, Lts Carroll and C. Smith, were lost in the same air battle between 12 Lightnings and five exceedingly good Messerschmitt pilots. In the hard blue above North Africa, the good guys did not always win.

In the end, they did. They did because they learned quickly and well; and because Eisenhower knew he was doing something wrong, and sent to England for General Carl Spaatz to tell him what it was.

America has possessed no greater air commander than General Spaatz. A World War I fighter pilot, credited with three air victories in France as CO of the 31st Aero Squadron, Spaatz commanded a pursuit group between wars, and went to England in 1942 to run the US 8th AF. He would later become Chief of the USAAF when General Arnold retired, and was the one man most responsible for creation of today's independent USAF.

When General Spaatz arrived in North Africa, he assessed the situation and then was characteristically brief and to-the-point in his recommendations to General Eisenhower. He said that fighter airplanes are poor defensive weapons; that airpower should always be used on the offensive, and that the first

Top right: Col Elliot Roosevelt, the President's son and CO of the 3rd PhG, discusses mission with Lt-Col Frank L. Dunn at La Senia. / *USAF*

Bottom right: P-38F-1, bearing Superman insignia, at Youks les Bains in December 1942. The 'UN' code was for the 94th FS, 1st FG. / *Kenneth M. Sumney*

Below: An F-4 Lightning of the 3rd Photographic Reconnaissance Group which arrived at La Senia, Algeria, in mid-December 1942. / *USAF*

mission of a tactical air force should be to win air superiority. Then, and only then, should it turn its attention to the supplementary roles required of it by an advancing ground force.

General Eisenhower gave Spaatz a free hand to do whatever was necessary.

That soon resulted in creation of the North-west African Air Forces (NAAF), headed by General Spaatz, and with a unified chain of command made up entirely of air officers. In late February 1943, NAAF was integrated into Air Chief Marshal Tedder's Mediterranean Air Command, which included, in North-east Africa, the Commonwealth Desert Air Forces and the US 9th AF under Air Vice-Marshal Coningham. Coningham's planes were bosses of the air over Libya as Montgomery pursued Rommel into Tunisia.

So, at last, all Allied air in North Africa was properly structured and efficiently directed. Time, God, and a little luck should take care of all else.

Time was a commodity in short supply within the USAAF Training Command, and replacement pilots for the decimated P-38 groups in North-west Africa often needed to rely on the other two above-mentioned factors.

A too typical product of those desperate days was Lt Norman W. Jackson, one of the first 26 replacement pilots that arrived with the 82nd FG just before Christmas 1942:

'I had only 30 hours in P-38s, and no aerial gunnery. Graduating from a bomber advanced school and being stationed at Olympia, Washington, for three months of fog and rain, had left something to be desired.

'Arriving in North Africa, we were put in combat with the 14th FG at a time when they were being terribly mauled by ground fire, as well as superior numbers of experienced German pilots.

'By the time I had 30 hours' combat, I had bailed out, crash-landed in the desert, returned home on one engine, and brought another P-38 home so shot up that it was junked.

'Being inept at gunnery was frustrating, but I finally managed two confirmed victories, one Fw190 head-on, holding the red dot on his yellow spinner almost too long and flying through the debris; and the other an Me109 from the rear, closing so fast that my props almost chewed him up before I broke off . . .'

Jackson's experiences not only underscore his own determination in the face of his several handicaps, but remind us again that the big fighter took pretty good care of its pilots.

It certainly took care of Capt Herbert Johnson of the 48th FS one day. While on a fighter sweep near Tripoli with seven other P-38s, Johnson spotted four enemy staff cars and four trucks between the border and Medenine in South-east Tunisia. The Lightnings had already shot up some other targets, but the cars looked important. Herb Johnson went in with all five guns firing and one car exploded; but his concentration on the target had crossed that fine line into

Above: Engine change. The national insignia was outlined in red on 48th FS machines while yellow outline was used by most others. / *Ervin Ethell*

Above centre: Lt William J. Hoelle of the 49th FS surveys damage to his P-38 *Maximum Goose* incurred when he struck a telephone pole during a strafing run, 31 December 1942. / *USAF*

Above left: General Carl A. 'Tooey' Spaatz (left), and Lt-Col Ralph Garman, CO of the 1st FG. / *Kenneth M. Sumney*

Bottom left: Lt Virgil H. Smith, 48th FS, 14th FG, scored five aerial victories during his first month in combat over North Africa. / *USAF*

Right: The airfield at Biskra, Algeria was home to the 301st Bomb Group, the 1st FG, and HQ for the 12th Bomber Command in January 1943. / *USAF*

Right: Lt Ervin C. Ethell of the 14th FG had four confirmed victories and a probable in a single action near Bizerte on 28 November 1942. / *Ervin Ethell*

Far right: Flak-damaged Lightning of the 48th FS (ES) apparently has national insignia outlined in red. Red photographs darker than blue on some old films. / *Ervin Ethell*

Below: This P-38F-15 of the 94th FS, 1st FG, struck a pole while strafing, but returned to base. / *Kenneth M. Sumney*

fixation, and Capt Johnson flew into the ground.

Lt Ervin Ethell, flying with Johnson, saw the horrendous cloud of dust and immediately retarded power to circle and see if his companion had, by chance, survived the crash. Then Ethell stared in disbelief as Johnson's P-38, minus one propeller and with is tail booms askew, came staggering out of the dust still flying. Nursing his speed carefully, Johnson actually coaxed his flying wreck to almost 8,000ft to clear the mountains between him and Youks les Baines. There, he landed wheels-up and walked away unhurt.

As good as Youks must have looked to Capt Johnson that day, it wasn't much of a place to return to. In addition to the poor food and primitive life style, Youks was periodically bombed and strafed by Ju88s; and on 9 January 1943, following a particularly heavy raid by the Luftwaffe, the 14th FG moved to Berteaux, about five miles

east of Telergma. The 1st FG was at Biskra, working with Bomber Command, and the 82nd FG would not have all its people together, and enough airplanes, to begin effective operations from Telergma until early February.

Between 9 January and 28 January, the 14th FG flew 23 missions (232 sorties) in response to 12th Fighter Command directives. On 23 January Maj Wade Walles led 16 Lightnings on a strafing mission to Gabes and Ben Gardine. Just short of Mendenine, the flight entered an overcast and broke out over the Luftwaffe field at Ben Gardine. The enemy was caught by surprise. There were a number of aircraft on the field, some in the landing pattern, and some taking-off. The P-38s bounced the planes that were airborne, about 20 in number.

Lt Yates made a pass only to find an Me109 on his tail, though it went down almost at once under the guns of Capt Ralph Watson. Other German fighters were hit, but there was no time to watch them strike the ground. In addition to the low-altitude dogfight, ground fire was intense. Lt Schottelkorb was seen to crash in flames. When the P-38s broke

off the 30-minute melée, low on fuel and ammunition, only 10 of them left the area.

Of the six missing pilots, Lt Mark Shipman would be the only one to make it back. Shipman crash-landed his badly damaged Lightning near Gafsa; was stripped of his belongings, except for a pair of pants, by local Arabs, and then proceeded to walk the 250 miles back to Berteaux, at one point in his journey passing through an Italian camp as if he belonged there.

On 28 January 1943 the 14th FG was taken out of combat. Of the original 54 pilots who participated in Operation Torch, 32 had been lost, 23 in aerial combat. In exchange, the 14th was credited with 62 enemy aircraft destroyed, seven probables, and 17 damaged, a proud record indeed when one considers that aerial combat was largely a by-product of the 14th's assigned role in North-west Africa.

With the departure of the 14th FG, there would be but two Lightning groups to fight in North-west Africa. The skeletonised 82nd FG had flown a few missions during January 1943 and, bolstered by the planes and replacement pilots left behind by the 14th, the 82nd was at least as strong as the group it

Right: Maj-Gen James Doolittle pins the Distinguished Flying Cross on Maj Wade C. Walles, CO of the 48th FS, February 1943. / *USAF*

Below: Ubiquitous entertainer Bob Hope was in North Africa in 1943 posing with P-38 pilots (left to right) Lts George Richards, John Meidinger, A. G. Barber, and Richard Jennings of the 14th FG. / *USAF*

Far right, top: A 94th FS Lightning at Biskra. *Ace, Daisy, Eunice,* and *Dick* are among the names painted on this one. / *Kenneth M. Sumney*

Far right, bottom: Lightnings of the 49th FS, 14th FG, approach Tunis on an armed reconnaissance mission. / *Ervin C. Ethell*

replaced. The 1st FG was moved to Chateaudun-du-Rhumel on 28 January to continue its service to Bomber Command.

On the 30th, 16 Lightnings of the 82nd's 96th squadron escorted B-25 Mitchells to El Aouinet, and in a running battle with Me109s, from Gabes to Chott Djerid, four P-38s were lost and six of the enemy went down. Most of these pilots were recently commissioned staff sergeant pilots, including Lt William J. Sloan credited with his first victory this day. Sloan would go on to become the 82nd FG's ranking ace with 12 official victories.

Meanwhile, the British 8th Army had chased Rommel all the way to Tunisia. By mid-February, the Afrika Korps linked up with the German and Italian forces at Medenine, and Rommel assumed overall command of the Axis forces in Tunisia. He established a strong defensive position on his eastern flank, known as the Mareth Line, to halt the British 8th Army, and then boldly attacked Eisenhower's forces to the west through the Kasserine Pass. This attack, intended to overrun Allied airfields and capture badly-needed fuel for German Panzer units, was turned back after eight days of heavy fighting. Every Allied airplane that could fly was committed to the battle, and even the B-17s were used in a tactical role at low altitudes.

Rommel, having found no weakness on his western flank, sent his Panzers in a series of four attacks against the British 8th Army on

Top right: Lt Mark Shipman, centre, upon his return to Berteaux after a 250-mile walk through enemy territory. At one point in his journey he strode boldly through an Italian encampment. / *Ervin C. Ethell*

Right: A 48th FS Lightning, P-38G-3 (one of only 12 built), at Youks les Bains. / *Ervin C. Ethell*

Below: Vision obscured by dust, two P-38 pilots of the 1st FG collided during take-off at Biskra; January 1943. / *USAF*

6 March. His losses were heavy, and he gained nothing.

Two weeks later, the British out-flanked the 20-mile-wide Mareth Line, forcing Rommel to retreat northward towards Tunis. Then on 7 April elements of the British 8th Army met Eisenhower's forces in North-central Tunisia. The two armies, that had started 1,700miles apart, had closed the pincer. Rommel was surrounded and backed against the sea.

But there was still a lot of fight left in the Desert Fox; exactly how much, would depend upon his aerial supply lines from Sicily and Italy. Allied intelligence sources soon reported that more than 500 air transports, Ju52s, SM82s, and Me323s, were based in Italy and Sicily, and that two daily runs were made across the narrow Sicilian Straits with strong fighter escort. The flights originated at Naples, staged through Sicily, and usually terminated at Sidi Ahmed or El Aouina. (We would later learn that during the four months from December to the end of March, the Germans airlifted more than 40,000 men and 14,000 tons of supplies to Africa.)

This great enemy airlift spawned Operation Flax, a coordinated Allied air offensive directed against the German transports and their bases.

Operation Flax began on 5 April 1943, with the 1st FG making an early morning sweep of the Mediterranean north of the Cape Bone-Bizerte area, while the 95th FS of the 82nd FG escorted Mitchells to Bo Rimzo Airfield in Sicily, and the 95th FS took another gaggle of Mitchells to look for enemy shipping in the Sicilian Straits north of Tunis. The P-40 units (there were five US Warhawk groups, along with seven RAF, RAAF, and SAAF Kittyhawk squadrons in North Africa) were given additional sweep and terminal attack missions. B-17s, escorted by the 31st FGs Spitfires, bombed the airfields at Sidi Ahmed and El Aouina.

The action began early, at 06.30hrs, when the 26 Lightnings from the 1st FG found 50 to 75 Ju52s and their fighter escorts north-east of Cape Bone. Attacking in pairs, with the advantage of altitude, the P-38s destroyed 11 of the Junkers transports, three Me109s, an Fw187, and two Ju87 Stukas. Two P-38s were lost.

Two hours later, the 20 Lightnings of the 96th FS, with a similar number of Mitchells in tow, discovered another enemy air convoy low above the Mediterranean in the same area. There were 40 to 70 Ju52s, with a mixed escort of four Ju87s, 10 Me109s, six Me110s an Me210, and an Fw190. The P-38s shared seven Ju52s with the Mitchells, then fought the Messerschmitts all the way to Cape Serrat, downing three Me109s, one Me110, the Me210, and three Ju87s. Four Lightnings went down in this running battle.

On the 10th, the 27th Squadron 1st FG flew top cover while the 71st Squadron ranged down to 100ft off the water to find the low-flying enemy transports over the Sicilian Straits. Again, at 06.30hrs near Cape Bone, the Lightnings came upon their quarry; 50 Ju52s, escorted by 15 Macchi C200s and Fw190s. This time, the P-38s shot down 28 of the enemy and lost none of their own.

Below: A 48th FS Lightning is serviced at Youks les Bains as C-47 supply planes arrived with mail, ammunition and food. / *Ervin C. Ethell*

The 82nd FG was up at 10.45hrs with 27 Lightnings escorting Mitchells on another sweep of the sea. At 12.40hrs they encountered 30 enemy transports with two Me110s, three Ju88s, and two Ju87s, 10 miles north of Cape Bone heading for Tunis. Eleven P-38s stayed with the Mitchells while the others attacked, shooting down 10 Ju52s, a Ju88, and an Me110. Lt W. L. Riddle, after getting a transport, ran upon the 110 so fast that he cut off its tail with his props, downing both himself and the enemy. Meanwhile, 15 Me109s joined the battle, and one of them was shot down before the P-38s, low on ammunition, dived for home. Lt Riddle was their only loss.

On the following day, the 82nd was low over the sea again with 19 Lightnings from the 95th FS, and 20 from the 96th FS. The 95th flew towards Sicily and met a formation of 20 enemy transports just above the water north of La Goulette with a cover of four Me110s and four or more Ju88s at 2,000ft along with seven or more Me109s somewhat higher. The P-38s got all of the transports on this occasion, including one that was believed to be a Ju252, and also shot down seven of the escorting fighters. Three Lightnings were lost, one of which, flown by Lt Grinnan, collided with a Ju52.

In the meantime, the 96th FS was mistakenly directed, and four of its four-plane elements missed the area where the action was. The remaining four aircraft, however discovered 25 to 30 Ju52s flying back to Sicily, 10 miles south of Maratina. The official report omits mention of fighter cover, but there apparently was some because one P-38 went down in exchange for five of the unarmed Ju52s.

We should mention that the P-40 units also participated very effectively in Flax. On 18 April, 47 Warhawks and 12 Spitfires staged the 'Palm Sunday Massacre' in which 58 Ju52s, 14 Me202s, and four Me109s were shot down for the loss of six Warhawks and one Spitfire. (Contrary to some off-the-cuff assessments in the past, the Warhawk/Kittyhawk was more than a match for the Me109G below 15,000ft.)

The success of Flax, predicated upon Allied countrol of the air over North Africa from mid March onward, wrote the final pronouncement for the Axis powers there. On 13 May 270,000 German and Italian soldiers, trapped on Tunisia's north coast and denied the means to make war, surrendered at last.

Field Marshal Rommel left North Africa shortly before the end, and would plague the Allies in Italy a bit later.

The 14th FG, at full strength with a new squadron added (37th FS), possessing 105 pilots and 90 new P-38Gs, returned to Telergma just before the enemy capitulated. This pioneer Lightning group would return to the thick of things in Italy.

The fighting 82nd would be there too, along with the 1st FG. The 82nd lost 64 Lightnings to down 199 enemy aircraft, plus 39 probables and 47 damaged since entering combat the previous December. But it was offered no respite. Pantelleria and Sicily were next, then the invasion of Italy.

Left: Capt Herbert E. Johnson, 48th FS, flew into the ground while strafing enemy vehicles on 31 December 1942, but brought his badly damaged Lightning back to base. / *Ervin C. Ethell*

South-West Pacific 1942-1943

Someone long ago observed that victory in war depends less upon the brilliance of a nation's leaders than upon the blunders of the enemy. Defeat is largely self-administered. A case in point is the Japanese attack on the US Naval base at Pearl Harbor on 7 December 1941. Nothing America's leaders could have said or done would have so united the country in a fierce determination to fight. A day before, the US Congress would have rejected war. A day after, few Americans would settle for less than the absolute, unconditional surrender of Japan and her Axis partners. The Japanese had made a blunder of monstrous proportions.

Japan's folly would not be apparent for a while because the United States was unprepared for war. For six months, the Nipponese would exult in one victory after another as they moved swiftly southward against the Philippines, Malaya, and Netherland's Indies. By the time the Philippines fell to the Japanese in early May 1942, the enemy also controlled Burma, Thailand, French Indochina, the Malay Archipelago, and farther to the east had secured strong lodgments on the islands of

New Guinea, New Britain, and in the Solomons, flanking the approaches to Australia and New Zealand from the United States.

Into this uncertain arena came the Lightning, a total of four of them, on 7 April 1942. These machines were F-4s, photo-reconnaissance versions of the P-38E. They were assigned to the 8th Photographic Squadron (which had no parent group) of the 5th Air Force, commanded by Maj Karl Polifka, and originally formed in Melbourne, Australia.

The 8th PhS was operational by mid-July, flying from Laloki and Port Moresby, New Guinea, just across the Owen Stanley Mountains from the Japanese.

The Battle of the Coral Sea in May had saved Port Moresby from invasion; and the Battle of Midway in June had reduced the enemy's aircraft carrier strength to the same level as America's (six each). These two battles had established the aircraft carrier as the new master of the seas. Therefore, in view of the vast distances encompassed by Japan's newly-won oceanic empire, and America's

Below: Slightly over 1,400 photo-reconnaissance Lightnings were produced. The first 500, built at Lockheed and designated F-4 to F-5B, employed airframes and engines of the P-38E to P-38J-10. The rest came from the Dallas Modification Center as re-worked J and L models. The F-5 above used P-38H-1 airframe. / *Guy Watson*

Left: Dean of Lightning recce pilots was Karl Polifka, who took the 8th PhS to the SW Pacific in April 1942, later served in Italy. / *USAF*

Below: Lightnings arrive in New Caledonia, November 1942, for the 339th FS on Guadalcanal. / *USAF*

capacity to far out-strip Japan in building and manning new carriers, it was clear that the enemy could not prevent the American occupation and build-up of forces on 'one damned island after another' across the South-west Pacific. These bases would insure the security of Australia and New Zealand, and provide the stepping stones to re-take the Philippines and, ultimately, strike at Japan herself.

Meanwhile, the Japanese must be dislodged from some of these islands, and on 7 July 1942 the US Joint Chiefs directed that Admiral Nimitz, commanding the Pacific Ocean Areas (North, Central, and South Pacific), begin a series of operations in the Solomons, advancing on the Japanese stronghold of Rabaul on New Britain Island in the Bismark Archipelago. Concurrently, General MacArthur, commanding the South-west Pacific Area, would move his Australian and American forces up the northern coast of New Guinea.

A stubborn enemy, however, would render these twin thrusts both costly and time-consuming.

In the meantime, Maj Polifka's 8th PhS mapped a large portion of eastern New Guinea and New Britain. The 8th's Lightnings were the only source of hard data on what the enemy was doing that MacArthur and Nimitz possessed. Their normal recon route was direct to Rabaul, then back to Port Moresby by way of enemy-occupied Lae and Salamaua on New Guinea's northeast coast.

Polifka and his 'Eight Balls,' as the squadron came to be known, regarded weather as a greater threat than the enemy fighters. Their Lightnings could out-run anything the Japanese had; but on the way to Rabaul the F-4s crossed the Equatorial Front and its quick-forming tropical storms. They had many bad moments with these.

The 8th's possession of the unarmed Lightnings led to some unusual incidents. Once, Lt Alex Guerry encountered four Rufe floatplanes during a low level run Angered because he had no guns, Guerry began to make passes at the slower craft, eventually forcing all of them to land. As the last Rufe settled on the water, Guerry dived again and 'swooshed him with my propeller wash,' flipping it on to its back. Guerry then photographed the scene to establish confirmation for his kill. As far as is known, it was the only enemy aircraft to be 'swooshed down' in combat.

However, Lt Robert Faurot of the 39th FS at Port Moresby 'splashed down' a Zero shortly afterwards. On 24 November the

Right: Admiral Chester Nimitz commanded Central and South Pacific Areas, including the 7th and 13th AFs which drove to meet MacArthur's Southwest Pacific forces, spearheaded by the 5th AF, to regain control of the Pacific and the air above it./ *US Navy*

Below: Brave photographer got this shot of 39th FS P-38s returning to Laloki (14-Mile Drome), Port Moresby, New Guinea late in 1942. Lightning at left, No 23, was usually piloted by Charles Sullivan. / *Australian War Memorial*

39th's Lightnings each took a 500lb bomb to the Japanese base at Lae. Faurot missed his target and his bomb exploded in the water directly ahead of a Zero that was taking off to intercept the P-38s. The Zero struck the huge column of water and crashed.

Although the first Lightnings with guns arrived in Brisbane in August 1942, to form the 39th FS of the 35th FG, the 39th was not operational until mid November because most of its P-38F-1s, 30 machines in all, had leaking inter-coolers, missing ammunition feeds, faulty inverters, and poorly-sealed fuel tanks. When all these problems were solved, the 39th moved to Laloki, Port Moresby's 14-mile Drome, with Capt George Prentice commanding.

In the meantime, the 339th FS of the 347th FG, on Henderson Field, Guadalcanal (in the Solomons, 850 miles east of Port Moresby) began receiving P-38s which it flew together with its P-39s. The 339th flew its first P-38 mission on 18 November, escorting five B-17s of the 11th BG on an attack against enemy shipping.

The 39th FS had its first big fight with the Japanese on 27 December when it scrambled 12 Lightnings to intercept 12 'Zekes', along with 12 'Vals' (Aichi D3A1-1, Type 99 dive bomber), escorted by 31 'Oscars' (Nakajima Ki-43, Type 1 fighter). The enemy formation appeared headed for the new Allied base at Dobodura.

The P-38s, led by Capt Thomas J. Lynch, found the enemy just beyond the mountains and scattered the Oscars by diving through their formation on a firing pass that carried the Lightnings down for a pass at the Vals, and then up again for another crack at the Oscars. By that time, the Zekes were entering the battle, and P-40s from the 9th FS arrived to get a piece of the action.

The relatively inexperienced P-38 pilots made mistakes. Some fired prematurely from extreme ranges; several wasted time and opportunity chasing friendly P-40s, and others slowed down and tried to dog-fight the agile Zekes on the enemy's terms. Still, the 39th FS's 12 Lightnings claimed nine victories without loss to themselves. Lt Richard I. Bong, flying a P-38 (although flying with the Warhawk equipped 9th FS, 49th FG), claimed a Val and a Zeke, his first victories. He would get more.

Four days later, the 39th FS destroyed nine more enemy fighters on a bomber support

Above: A 39th FS Lightning at Port Moresby, early in 1943.
/ Steve Birdsall via Bruce Hoy

67

mission to Lae. Lt Ken Sparks got one of them when he sheared-off its right wing in a collision. Sparks lost two feet of his own right wing, but returned safely to Laloki.

On 4 January 1943 the 9th FS, 49th FG, received the first of its Lightnings, and two days later, when the 8th PhS's F-4s reported an enemy convoy headed for the Japanese base at Lae, New Guinea, the 9th's P-38s joined all other Allied aircraft at Port Moresby in the attack. The Lightnings and Warhawks shot down more than 50 enemy aircraft during the three-day battle (Dick Bong added two to his score in his brand new P-38G).

At this time, General Kenney's 5th AF fighter commander, General Paul 'Squeeze' Wurtsmith, possessed but 330 fighter aircraft, only 80 of which were P-38s. Another 72 were P-400 (P-39) Airacobras, employed almost exlusively for ground attack missions since they were so clearly inferior to Japanese fighters, while most of the rest were P-40 Warhawks and Kittyhawks. Among the latter were seven Royal New Zealand Air Force squadrons, eight Royal Australian Air Force squadrons, and one Dutch squadron. Since the P-40 had neither the range nor altitude capability of the P-38, General Kenney's on-going pleas for more P-38s is understandable.

A lull in the air action followed the early January battles, with enemy aircraft appearing in force only once during February; then, on 1 March the Japanese dispatched eight transports with eight

68

destroyers to land 6,000 troops at Lae. This resulted in the Battle of the Bismark Sea, which was primarily fought between the Japanese and the 5th Air Force.

On the 2nd, in marginal weather, 16 Lightnings of the 9th and 39th FSs were sent with 28 Flying Fortresses to attack the ships in Huon Gulf. One transport was sunk and the P-38s downed two Oscars. On the following day the weather was clear, and 28 Lightnings accompanied the B-25s, A20s, and Australian Beaufighters to the Lae area. The P-38s claimed nine enemy fighters destroyed out of 25, but lost Bob Faurot and two others from the 39th FS. Dick Bong got his sixth confirmed victory (which he called an 'Oscar-type Zero' in his report. Many American airmen tended to call all Japanese fighters 'Zeros'), and Lt Harry Brown, who had shot down two Japanese planes over Pearl Harbor on 7 December 1941, flying a P-36 Hawk, was credited with another.

Meanwhile, the Beaufighters, A-20s and Mitchells, skip-bombing and strafing, sent two destroyers and three transports to the bottom. PT boats sank the last transport. Of the 16-ship convoy, only four destroyers

Above: Insignia of the 339th FS.

Top left: Walter Beane, Australian intelligence officer, talks with pilots of the 39th FS before the P-38F flown by Dick Bong at that time. / *Charles W. King*

Left: Lt Robert Faurot, 39th FS, 35th FG, who 'sunk' an enemy fighter plane to make the first P-38 kill in the SW Pacific. / *Curran L. 'Jack' Jones*

Right: A 9th FS Lightning near Port Moresby, 8 March 1943. / *Bruce Hoy*

Above: Lightnings of the 9th FS, 49th FG, at Dobodura. The 9th was equipped with P-38s in January 1943. / *Australian War Memorial*

Right: US airmen in the SW Pacific dropped surrender invitations over enemy hold-outs without noticeable results. / *Richard Bracey*

Far right, top: In January 1943 the 17th PhS was operating from Cactus Strip on Guadalcanal. The F-5A-1 above, s/n 42-12670, was finally retired at Biak in August 1945 after 200 missions and 1,019 hours' flying time. / *Dr Richard Burns*

Far right, bottom: Camera control of recce Lightning. Diving speed limits were affixed to control column. / *USAF*

survived, rescuing about 2,700 enemy soldiers and returning them to Rabaul.

It was not a large battle by World War II standards, but it was a significant one. Taken together with the final victory on Guadalcanal the previous November, it greatly facilitated American strategy in the Pacific. In this strategy the two lines of advance, the one, under Nimitz, across the Central Pacific via the Gilberts, Marshall,s Marianas, Carolines, and Palaus toward the Philippines; and the other, under MacArthur, in the South-west Pacific via the north coast of New Guinea to the Vogelkop and thence to the southern Philippines, were mutually supporting, and forced Japan to spread her defence forces thinly, especially, as Allied forces in India gathered for an assault from another quarter.

Late in March, the 80th FS of the 8th FG transitioned to P-38s and joined the 9th and 39th FSs at Port Moresby. That made three P-38 squadrons in the 5th AF, each from a different group.

Then, between 2 and 18 April, Japanese Admiral Isoruku Yamamoto's entire carrier air fleet was land-based at Rabaul for Operation I-go, an all-out attempt to regain air superiority over eastern New Guinea and the Solomons. These forces made two major raids against Allied bases on New Guinea with as many as 100 aircraft, hitting Port Moresby on the 12th, and Milne Bay on the 14th. The enemy lost 32 bombers and 23 fighters, largely to the P-38s.

But the show-down air battles never took place. Operation I-go was abruptly terminated when P-38s of the 347th FG on Guadalcanal ambushed Admiral Yamamoto.

★ ★ ★ ★ ★ ★ ★ ★

Surrender Pass

The bearer is surrendering. He is to be treated courteously and escorted to the rear.

COMMANDING OFFICER
OF THE U. S. FORCES

戰線通過査證

本票所持ノ者ハ自發投降者ナ
リ。丁重ニ同人ヲ取扱ヒ、後方
ニ護送スベシ。

米國軍司令官

米軍陣地ニテ此ノ票ヲ示セ!

Above: On 5 April 1943 Clay Tice's P-38 suffered a collapsed nose wheel strut in soft ground at Dobodura, New Guinea. Tice would go through a number of P-38s called *Elsie* until at last setting down on Japanese soil, as CO of the 49th FG, in August 1945. / *USAF*

Right: Personnel of the 475th FG examine one of their new P-38Hs at Townsville, Australia, May 1943. The 475th was the first all-Lightning group in the SW Pacific, and one of the hottest fighter outfits of the war. / *Frank F. Smith*

Top right: P-38Fs. / *Lockheed Aircraft Corporation*

Bottom right: P-322 (Lightning Mk1) USAAF trainer. / *USAF*

Overleaf: P-38M Night Lightning. / *USAF*

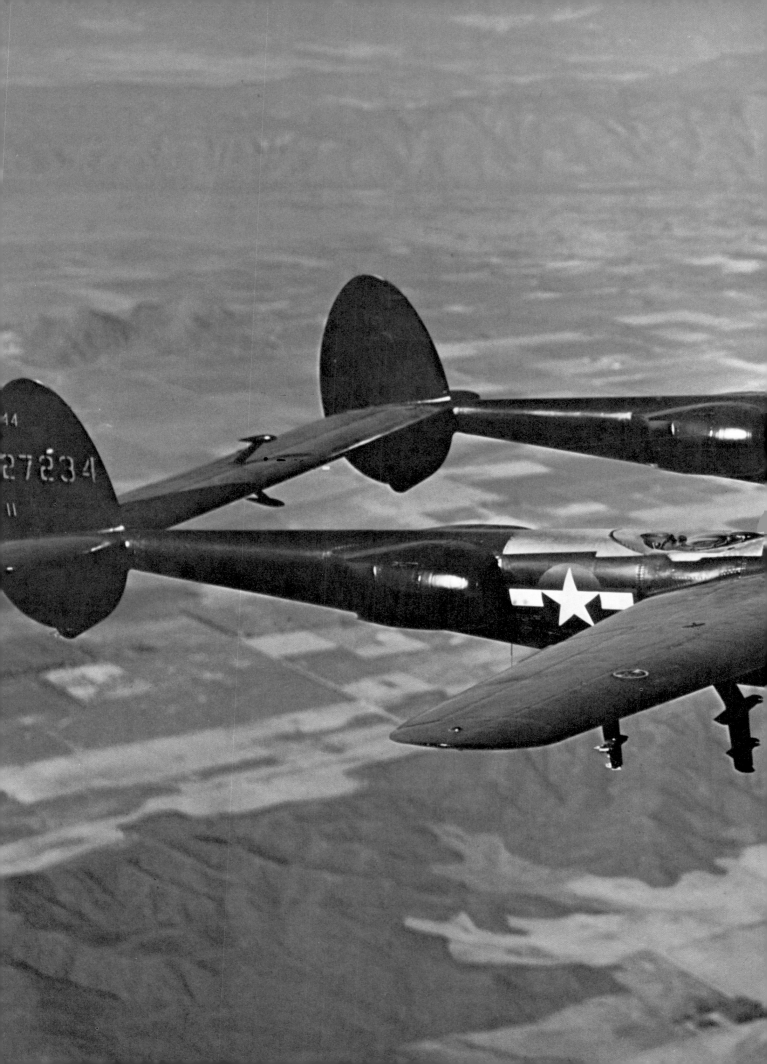

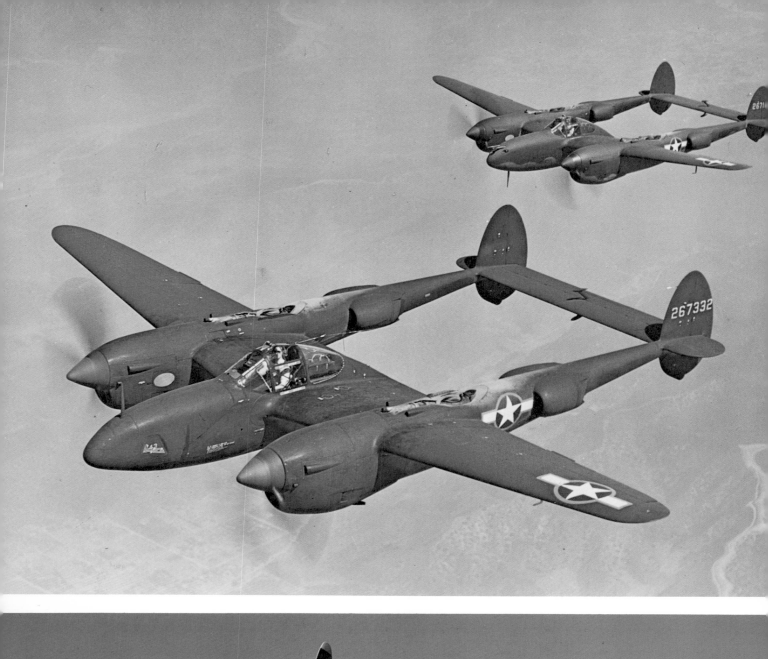

During the preceding two weeks, the 347th FG (339th and 70th FSs; still the only P-38s in the Solomons) had also taken its toll of enemy aircraft as they came down the 'slot' from Rabaul, as many as 160 Vals and Zeros on a single raid. However, the 347th's most significant mission was its assignment to kill an admiral, the Commander of the Japanese Fleet, and perhaps his country's most brilliant strategist.

It was possible because US Navy cryptographers had broken the enemy's naval code (which earlier provided the key to the American victory at Midway). Admiral Nimitz was reading his enemy's mail. And when a message was intercepted informing that Admiral Yamamoto would leave Rabaul aboard a 'Betty' (Mitsubishi G4M1 Navy attack plane) on 18 April for an inspection trip to Ballale, Bougainville, 16 Lightnings were hurriedly serviced for the intercept.

Two P-38s aborted the mission with mechanical problems, leaving 10 to take care of Yamamoto's fighter escort, while four Lightnings would go after the Admiral's plane.

Yamamoto left Rabaul precisely on time in a 705th Kokutai Betty accompanied by Admiral Ugaki in a second Betty and escorted by six Zeros of the 309th Kokutai.

At 09.34hrs, Doug Canning spotted the Japanese formation, dead on course and only one minute from estimated interception: 'Bogeys, eleven o'clock high!' The Lightnings separated, climbing steeply. Lt Besby Holmes momentarily turned away from the attack until he could free his drop tanks, and his wing man, Lt Ray Hine, followed him. That left Capt Thomas Lanphier and Lt Rex Barber to make the initial pass at the Bettys.

Lanphier was a mile east of the Japanese formation when he saw the Zeros' drop tanks flutter away. The Zeros turned into the P-38s and Lanphier flamed one in a head-on pass as Barber followed a Betty to treetop level. Three Zeros were on Barber's tail, but were driven off by Holmes and Hine.

Above: Crew chief Willard Berg checks the Form One of this 347th FG Lightning from the comfort of his homemade 'beach chair.' / *USAF*

Top left: An F-5B-1 with a P-38J-5 behind. / *Lockheed Aircraft Corporation*

Bottom left: P-38G-10. / *USAF*

73

Lanphier had rolled on to his back to look out the top of his canopy for the Bettys, and saw Barber with two Zeros and the lead Betty 'skimming along the surface of the jungle headed for Kahili.' He dived on the Betty, with two Zeros chasing desperately, and began firing at extreme range. At this point, Holmes and Hine scattered the Zeros (actually three, though Lanphier saw but two) closing on Barber, and Barber switched his attention to the second Betty which was turning out to sea close to the surface. Lanphier slowed, coolly concentrating on his gunsight, and sent another long burst into the lead Betty. Flames erupted from its right engine, its right wing tore away, and it crashed into the jungle. Lanphier turned into the Zeros following him, and entered a shallow high-speed climb, out-distancing the enemy fighters.

While the remaining Lightnings were busy with additional Zeros swarming up from the field at nearby Kahili, Homes and Hine again rescued Barber who was pursuing the second Betty low over the water, raking it with his guns and cannon, as he himself was again bracketed by three Zeros. Holmes came down with his air speed indicating 425mph and flamed two of the Zeros as Hine went after the third. Holmes' momentum carried him past Barber to close very fast on the Betty. He eased-in the rudder to frame the enemy in the lighted ring of his gunsight, and fired an unusually long burst into the Betty's right engine. In his eagerness, Holmes almost crashed into his target before diving beneath it with only a few feet to spare above the water. He looked back to see the Betty explode as it struck the surface.

Above: Lightnings of the 39th FS just prior to their first air battle with Japanese fighters on 27 December 1942. No 33 was normally flown by Ken Sparks or Richard Smith. */ Bruce Hoy*

Left: Maj Frank Savage, who succeeded Polifka as commander of the 8th PhS, 'dines informally' from atop fuel drum at Port Moresby. */ USAF*

Above: On 16 June 1943 Lt Murray Schubin of the 339th FS destroyed five enemy fighters and claimed a sixth as a probable during a 45-minute air battle. / *USAF*

It appears the both Barber and Holmes claimed the second Betty, from which Vice Admiral Ugaki miraculously escaped. Capt Lanphier was credited with downing the lead Betty in which Admiral Yamamoto died. Ray Hine did not return from the mission, the only loss suffered by the attacking force.

Throughout the summer of 1943 the 347th FG's two squadrons continued to meet the enemy with success disproportionate to their dwindling strength. By August, only a few P-38s were left in the Solomons, and the P-40s along with Marine Corsair squadron VMF-124, would necessarily carry much of the fighters' burden until more Lightnings were available to the 13th AF.

Actually, 115 new P-38G Models came out of the Eagle Farms Depot at Brisbane in May; but General Kenney got them for service in New Guinea with his 5th AF. Kenney used them to form the 475th FG. He chose Maj George Prentice of the 39th FS as the 475th's commander, and Prentice raided the 39th and 80th FSs for squadron and element leaders. The 475th would consist of the 431st, 432nd,

and 433rd FSs. At long last there would be an all-Lightning group in the Pacific.

The 5th AF also received, a few weeks later, the 348th FG, commanded by Maj Neel E. Kearby, and equipped with P-47 Thunderbolts.

The reason for the 5th AF's sudden wealth in fighter airplanes was soon apparent. In June, General MacArthur and Vice Admiral Halsey, Nimitz's commander in the South Pacific, resumed their offensive to encircle Rabaul. By early August Army forces under Halsey secured New Georgia, with its important Munda airfield, in the central Solomons; and by 1 November US Marines were on Bouganville, just 300 miles southeast of Rabaul.

MacArthur's forces (mostly Australian) meanwhile advanced up the north-east coast of New Guinea to occupy Salamaua, Lae, and the inland airfield at Nadzab, about 450 miles south-west of Rabaul.

In each phase of these twin campaigns, the Japanese sought unsuccessfully to contest Allied air and naval supremacy, losing in

Above: A bootleg in-flight photo of a 432nd FS P-38H en route to Wewak, August 1943.
/ *C. J. Rieman*

Left: On 15 October 1943 Charles MacDonald commandeered this 433rd FS Lightning to lead the 475th FG against a large enemy force approaching Oro Bay. MacDonald shot down two enemy planes, but his P-38 was damaged and he crash-landed at Dobodura.
/ *Teddy Hanks*

those efforts planes and pilots that they could ill afford to spare.

The new 475th FG entered combat in mid August 1943 when the 431st and 432nd FSs moved up to Twelve-Mile Strip and Ward's Drome at Port Moresby, and the 433rd went to Jackson Drome.

On 17 August, the 5th AF began an intensive five-day attack on the Wewak area to knock out enemy air opposition to Allied landings there scheduled for 4 September. Caught by surprise, the Japanese lost more than half their airplanes on the ground to Kenney's bombers on the first day. On succeeding days, P-38s of the 9th, 39th, and 80th FSs, along with those of the 475th FG, destroyed in air combat most of those that remained. Salamaua fell to Australian troops on 13 September, Lae and Nadzab three days later; and by early October the 5th AF was concentrated at Dobodura in preparation for an all-out assault on Rabaul in concert with General Harmon's 13th AF in the Solomons.

The air offensive against Rabaul began 12 October with 106 Lightnings from all 5th AF units escorting 107 Liberators, Mitchells, and Beaufighters over the target area. Throughout the rest of October and into November, the strikes continued against the enemy, 100,000 strong, at Rabaul. The bomber groups went in turn, but the P-38s went every time. The 9th and 80th FSs received Distinguished Unit Citations for their outstanding performance in protecting the bombers while sharing a total of 50 confirmed kills.

In the end, no Allied forces were put ashore to take Rabaul. Possessing control of the air, MacArthur and Halsey seized strategically located islands to encircle the important stronghold, and left it to wither for the lack of supply.

The 80th FS field at Kila, Port
Moresby, 14 September 1943. P-38
in centre is *Ruff Stuff*, with 'X'
identifier on fin; *Porky* is at left,
with 'A' on fin. / *USAF*

Far left: One of the outstanding fighter leaders of the Pacific War was Capt Daniel T. Roberts who led the 433rd FS until his death on 9 November 1943, at which time he had 15 confirmed aerial victories. / *Dennis Glen Cooper*

Left: Top ace of the 80th FS, with 22 victories, was Jay T. Robbins, a cool and skilful fighter pilot who talked sparingly. / *John Stanaway*

Below left: Commanding Officer of the 475th FG was Lt-Col George Prentice, a former 39th FS commander. C/n faintly visible on nose of his Lightning identifies it as a P-38H-5. / *Dennis Glen Cooper*

Right: The 39th FS CO Thomas J. Lynch was another with unusual leadership abilities. Lynch was killed in March 1944, at which time he had 20 official victories. / *Australian War Memorial*

Below: Dick Bong with his 9th FS Lightning just after his 21st victory on 5 November 1943. / *Carl Bong*

Sicily and Italy

Top right: 94th FS Lt J. Hagenback on airstrip at Sardinia with his bat-nosed P-38H-5 in October 1943. / *Bill Lenhart via Ken Sumney*

Bottom right: In mid-1943, the US transferred four F-4s and two F-5As to the French Groupe de Reconnaissance 2/33 then based in Tunisia. Later in the war, the French unit received F-5Bs (above). / *USAF*

Below: In September 1943, the Lightnings of the 12th AF began to operate from Sicily under conditions that harkened back to the early days in North Africa. Above, a 94th FS P-38G returns to base. / *USAF*

Following the Allied victory in North Africa in May 1943, planning proceeded for the invasion of Sicily (Operation Husky) according to decisions reached by Prime Minister Churchill and President Roosevelt at the January 1943 Casablanca Conference.

Neutralisation of the Luftwaffe was, of course, an essential prelude to the invasion, and during June the North-west African Air Forces crippled most of the enemy airfields in Sicily, destroying almost 1,000 planes. By 10 July, the day of the invasion, the remaining enemy aircraft had been moved to bases in Italy, and the ship convoys carrying 160,000 men, the British 8th Army and US 7th Army, discharged their cargoes with little enemy air opposition.

During the invasion, the Allied air umbrella extended far into Italy, and by 13 July, 12th AF fighters were making themselves at home on Sicilian airfields. German ground forces, however, held out for nearly three weeks, then escaped across the Straits of Messina to Italy under cover of darkness.

All this prompted the Italian king to force the resignation of Premier Mussolini and begin secret negotiations with the Allies to take Italy out of the war. Although the Italians were virtual prisoners of the 26 German divisions in their country, Italy's surrender was nevertheless announced by General Eisenhower on 8 September as the US 5th Army prepared to storm the beaches at Salerno. Five days earlier, British forces under Montgomery had crossed the Strait of Messina and landed in Southern Italy.

These dramatic developments were, however, only a beginning. The Germans' determined stand in Italy, under Field Marshal Kesselring, would continue for 20 difficult months and precipitate many great air battles.

During June, the three P-38 groups, the 1st, 14th and 82nd, were based in Tunisia. Also Lightning-equipped were the veteran 3rd PhG, re-designated Photographic Group Reconnaissance (PhGr), and the French Groupe de Reconnaissance 2/33 which had received four refurbished F-4s and two new F-5s.

Famed author Antoine de Saint-Exupery, at age 45, was a pilot in 2/33, which was commanded by Maj Rene Gavoille. These recce units, including RAF 682 Squadron, constituted the Mediterranean Allied Photo Reconnaissance Wing (MAPRW) under the command of Col Karl Polifka (succeeding Col Elliot Roosevelt) who had flown the first Lightning recce missions of the war in the SW Pacific.

Saint-Exupery would be one of the many lone recce pilots that failed to return from a mission and whose manner of death was never known.

But the very fact that the recce pilots had no guns led them to temptations that other combat pilots would not usually entertain. Before Sardina was taken, Col Frank Dunn dived through a low overcast near Cagliari to find himself in the midst of circling enemy aircraft over an Axis airfield. Dunn joined them 'because I didn't want to be conspicuous.' The uncertain enemy pilots merely stared at him. None fired. At last

Right: Maj Bill Leverette, CO of the 37th FS, 14th FG, led eight Lightnings against 25 Stukas, with Ju88 escorts, which were attacking British shipping near the Dodecanse Islands on 9 October 1943. Leverette shot down seven of the enemy, and the other P-38 pilots, including Bob Margison (right), accounted for 10 more.
/ *Bob Margison*

Below: Lt Richard Campbell of the 14th FG would later add one more swastika to the victory symbols on the nose of *Earthquake McGoon*. The Italian symbol was for an Mc202.
/ *USAF*

Dunn saw his chance to break away and continued over the city.

He arrived at the railway station just as a train was pulling in. He had some empty fuel tanks it was time to jettison, so he dropped lower and cut them loose over the train. The tanks struck the roof of the car just back of the locomotive and Dunn saw the engineer bailing out of his cab while passengers tumbled from the train's windows. It was a very satisfying sight.

By 13 August the Sicilian operation was going so well that the 12th AF sent 106 Fortresses, escorted by 45 Lightnings, along with 106 Marauders and 66 Mitchells, escorted by 90 Lightnings, to the marshalling yards at Littoria and Lorenzo near Naples. This involved most of the Lightnings available in the theatre, which were during this period mostly P-38G-10s and G-15s.

Near the target this force was intercepted by 75 enemy fighters, but the P-38s stayed with the bombers so well that only two Marauders were lost. Five enemy fighters were claimed.

Up to 17 August, when Operation Husky ended, all three P-38 groups carried out extensive fighter sweeps, raiding the enemy's evacuation routes, strafing trains, bombing railway tracks, attacking motor transports, knocking-out radar sites, and destroying

bridges. The 5th Photo Reconnaissance Group (PRG), equipped with F-5 Lightnings, joined the 12th AF at this time as the raids were concentrated in the Naples-Foggia area.

A maximum effort was ordered for the 1st and 82nd FGs on 25 August, directed against the airfields at Foggia; both groups would earn Distinguished Unit Citations for their execution of that mission. Every field at Foggia was to be hit, the 1st FG striking at fields 1, 2, and 4 with 65 Lightnings, while the 82nd FG would attack the rest with as many airplanes as they could muster.

The two groups were airborne at 07.06hrs, and approached the target area on a course of 270 degrees, all aircraft hugging the deck. They achieved total surprise. At 09.25hrs a deadly scythe of Lightnings cut across the broad plain, and was almost gone before there was any answering fire from the ground. In their wake, the P-38s left nearly 200 enemy aircraft destroyed or damaged. Two P-38s went down.

Despite their losses, the German and Italian fighters met the P-38s in large numbers on every raid. On 2 September, just a day before Montgomery crossed the Strait of Messina into Italy, the 82nd FG sent 74 P-38Gs and five P-38Fs to accompany 72 Mitchells to the Cancellor marshalling yards just north of Naples. This mission would result in another

Above left: Picture of a happy ace: Lt William J. 'Dixie' Sloan of the 82nd FG has just completed his tour in Italy with 12 victories, making him the top scorer in the 12th AF. Later, Michael Brezas of the 14th FG, 15th AF, would have a total of 12, and Maj Leverette would have 11. Photo is dated 9 August 1943, and Sloan's machine is a P-38G-10. */National Archives*

Above: Col Troy Keith, CO of the 14th FG, and a principal reason for the group's outstanding record. */USAF*

85

DUC for the 82nd. Lt Tom Jones flew one of the Lightnings:

'The Germans and Italians first put up about 70 fighters, Macchi 202s, Reggiane 2001s, and Me109s. As we approached at about 14,000ft from the sea, we could see the dust trails made by their take-offs from several fields.'

The confrontation developed into a savage running battle and, Jones continues:

'Never before or since have I seen so many aircraft in one area in combat. What an air battle! A total of 220 aircraft, of which 145 were fighters!

'We were using our escort formation that consisted of flights of four P-38s in trail, scissoring with four other four-plane elements above and around the B-25s when they hit us. Everywhere one looked a P-38 or an enemy fighter was in a steep dive or spiral, some smoking, to plunge into the Bay of Naples or the adjacent sea.

'Of course, we had to drop our two 165-gallon pylon tanks immediaterly, and it was 350 miles over water back to home base. Talk about gas rationing and leaning-out. They followed us out to almost 100 miles from Naples. Some of us couldn't make it—headed for the 31st American Spitfire strip on the north coast of Sicily to refuel... I got an Me109, right on the deck, not 100 yards away, crossing in front of me. The battle had worked down to just above the surface of the sea...'

The 82nd FG lost 10 P-38s that day. The Group downed 16 Me109s, five Macchi

86

C202s, one Reggiane 2001, one Fw190, and one unidentified fighter destroyed in a collision. In addition, five Me109s were listed at probables, and eight as damaged. The price was high, but all of the Mitchells returned safely.

On 9 September 1943, six days after Montgomery landed in extreme southern Italy, the US 5th Army, under General Mark Clark, staged an assault landing on beaches near Salerno, 25 miles south-east of Naples. The Germans reacted so violently that the issue on the ground was in doubt for a week, while the Luftwaffe struck at the beachhead with up to 100 planes at a time.

Once again, the P-38s were called in as the Allies' top guns. The recent air offensive had reduced P-38 strength in the theatre to less than 250 machines, spread among the three Lightning groups; but also available were two groups of A-36 Mustangs, one group of US Spitfires, and 18 squadrons of RAF Spitfires. It was barely enough, and every serviceable Allied fighter was ordered to fly two sorties per day. Escort, strafing, and bombing missions were flown in a seemingly endless procession, including another sweep of the Foggia airfields on 18 September that destroyed almost 300 enemy airplanes and gliders, until 27 September when the Foggia fields were occupied by the 8th Army. Three days later, the US 5th Army was in Naples, and the P-38 groups enjoyed a brief respite.

With Italy's surrender, about 225 Italian aircraft were flown to Sicily by their pilots to join the Allies. They were held out of combat until Italy officially declared war on Germany on 13 October. Then, three days later, Italian pilots flying Macchi C205s flew top cover for the 82nd FG as it dive-bombed enemy shipping in Levkas Channel.

Meanwhile, Italian pilots who remained sympathetic to the Axis cause were incorporated into a German fighter squadron (II/JG 77) with their Macchi C205s to form I Italian Fighter Group. The possibility of Italian versus Italian, in identical aircraft, thus existed.

On 1 November 1943 the US 15th AF was formed in Italy, with the Foggia airfields as its principal home. General Doolittle was the 15th's first commander, though General Nathan Twining soon took over when Doolittle went to England. All of the Lightnings in the theatre were transferred to the new 15th AF, the 1st, 14th, and 82nd FGs, as well as the 5th Photo Recon Group.

The German ground forces had fallen back to strong defensive positions anchored on towering peaks around the town of Cassino, some 90 miles south of Rome. This was the 'Winter Line', and the enemy would hold it throughout the winter and into the spring of 1944. Jack Lenox of the 49th FS, 14th FG, recalls:

'During this time, a lot of our missions were strafing and dive-bombing in support of the troops at Anzio. On 22 January 1944 British and American troops landed at Anzio, 60 miles behind the Winter Line; but the Germans kept them confined to the beachhead area throughout the winter. They couldn't break-out. It was all they could do to hold on.

Top left: In June 1944, the shuttle missions to Russia began when Lt Everett Thies flew his F-5C-1 Lightning into the USSR and back. With Thies is his crew chief, T/Sgt Daniel Noble. / *USAF*

Bottom left: Russians come to gape at the F-5 *Dot Dash.* A month later, General D. C. Strother, 306th Fighter Wing Commander, led 70 15th AF Lightnings and 50 Mustangs to Russia and back on a grand fighter sweep. /*USAF*

Below: Lt Thomas W. Smith, 37th FS, 14th FG, collided almost head-on with an Me109 on 16 January 1944. The 109's wing was sheared off; the P-38 lost an engine and suffered a severed tail but returned to base for a wheels-up landing. / *Bob Margison*

'Our route to the target area was from our airfield at Foggia across Italy to Naples, out to sea, and up the coast to Anzio. We returned the same way. But one day we decided to take a short-cut home and we ran into very heavy and uncomfortably accurate flak. Lt Paul Wingert got it in both engines and had to bail out. He had his problems on the way down with tangled shroud lines and a streaming parachute, but managed to get the canopy opened at a very low altitude.

'Now, Paul didn't see it, but below was an American infantry squad that, after days in the mud with nothing but cold rations, was queueing-up for a hot meal. Paul landed at the head of the chow line just as the cook yelled, "Come and get it!" Though a bit shaken Paul looked about him, his face blossomed into a smile, he picked up a mess kit and proceeded to be the first one through the chow line.'

During February, the 15th AF in Italy and the 8th AF in England began to co-ordinate mass air attacks deeper and deeper into Germany. The ground war in Italy was bogged down, but the long-legged P-38s could range well into Europe from Foggia, especially, after the P-38Js began arriving in March.

The P-38J models were significantly superior to all previous Lightnings. Powered with V-1710-89/91 engines of 1,325hp (1,600hp war emergency), the J had a maximum speed of 420mph at 25,000ft and an initial climb-rate, with military load, of

Left: Crew chief 'Gracie' Allen helps 14th FG CO Obie Taylor strap into *Pat III* for a mission. / *Oliver B. Taylor*

Right: Flag ship of the 14th FG at Foggia, Italy mid-1944. Group CO Taylor taxis down the PSP. Group emblem is on left engine nacelle. / *Oliver B. Taylor*

Below: New P-38J-15 at Mateur, Tunisia in late February 1944, on its way to the 1st FG at Foggia, Italy. / *Kenneth M. Sumney*

3,900fpm which eroded less than 25 per cent through 25,000ft. The J was the first Lightning with adequate cockpit heating, and with circuit breakers to cure its electrical ills. The P-38J-10 and onward possessed flat, bulletproof windscreens and, beginning with the P-38J-25s, hydraulic aileron boost and electrically-activated dive brakes were added. Weighing 13,700lb empty, and up to 24,000lb loaded, these Lightnings had a normal range of 2,300miles with 1,010gal (US) of fuel. Here at last, was the Lightning for all seasons, and all missions.

On 2 April the three P-38 groups in Italy were able to test substantially their new J models against the Luftwaffe. The mission called for the largest aerial force yet assembled in the theatre, to bomb the ball-bearing plant and aircraft factory at Steyr, Austria, with 450 heavy bombers.

The 82nd FG provided initial escort for the bombers and was jumped at 10.15hrs by 50 Me109s, Fw190s and Macchi 202s which attacked at bomber level, head-on, eager to engage the Lightnings. Another formation of enemy aircraft was stalking at 35,000ft clearly hoping to see the P-38s drawn away from the bombers. But the 82nd stuck to it, and got three Messerschmitts in the bargain.

Picking up the bombers at 10.45hrs, Thunderbolts of the 325th FG (the famed 'Checkertails,' who had flown Warhawks in North Africa) flew shotgun for the 'Big Friends' almost to the target, warding off another attack by 21 Me109s. Then, at 11.30hrs, the 1st FG arrived to take over the escort duty and was in turn obliged to deal with 70 enemy fighters in the target area.

Above: Lt Herbert B. Hatch points to the results of his battle with Fw190s on 10 June 1944, in which he shot down five 190s in a single 180-degree turn. He was, however, the only 71st FS pilot to return to base that day. The battle occurred over Ploesti. / *USAF*

Left: Lt-Col Ben A. Mason Jr, Deputy Group Commander, 82nd FG, put his bomb on the target at Ploesti, strafed flak batteries, destroyed two locomotives, and shot down an Me110 on that costly 10 June raid. / *Ben Mason*

Above: Small World Dept: Lt Tom Maloney, an eight-victory ace of the 27th FS, 1st FG, recalled that co-author's father, Ervin Ethell (14th FG), taught gunnery to Maloney at Lomita AAB. / *W. H. Caughlin*

Left: General Nathan Twining listens as Lt Richard T. Andrews tells how he landed in enemy territory to pick-up another 82nd FG pilot who had crash-landed. Capt Richard Willsie rode home on the lap of Andrews. / *Ben Mason*

Above: A Lightning of the 96th FS, 82nd FG, drops its bombs. On the Ploesti raid of 10 June 1944 the 82nd escorted by the 1st FG, attacked the oil refineries and met overwhelming opposition. The 82nd traded eight P-38s for three of the enemy; the 1st FG lost 14 Lightnings for claims of 20 German fighters. / *USAF*

Centre right: Lightnings of the 27th FS, 1st FG, in the classic 'Finger-Four' standard tactical formation. Two near planes are J-15s, in background are two L-1 models. S/ns are: 42-104428, 43-28650, 44-24379, and 44-24217. / *Warren Campbell*

Bottom right: By mid-August 1944 some P-38L-1s were arriving in Italy. This one belonged to the 94th FS, 1st FG. / *Francis J. Pope*

92

At that point, ruffles and flourishes would have been appropriate, because the 14th FG came charging in for its rendezvous with the bombers and joined the battle. With 80 Lightnings of the 1st and 14th fighting together, only six of the enemy fighters managed to get through to the bombers, and two of those were destroyed, two damaged, by P-38s of the 49th FS.

At 12.05hrs, as the first box of bombers came off the target, 40 Me110s and Me210s, with single-engine fighter escort, came in to release rockets, flying four abreast in successive waves. Elements of the 48th FS forced the twin-engine craft to break formation, pursued, and destroyed 12 of them in a 20-minute running battle.

In the interim, the 37th FS, which had taken over top cover protection of the bombers, destroyed six of the enemy, damaged one, and scored two probables without sacrificing position.

As the enemy broke-off the engagement, the 14th FG regrouped and stayed with the bombers until reaching a point just south of Klagenfurt. There, with no losses to count, but fuel gauges pointing below the prudence level, they returned to Foggia. The Lightning pilots were mightily pleased with their new machines, particularly Lt Robert Siedman who exulted, 'Boy, I'll bet Hitler would be real mad if he knew that a little Jewish boy had shot down three of his pilots today!'

Similar missions followed throughout April and May of 1944, and the effect on the defending forces is apparent when Luftwaffe

records for those dates are examined. JG 27 and IV/JG 77, responsible for the air defence of the Austrian sector, had but 124 single-engine fighters among them at the end of May, only 79 of which were operational. By that time the 15th AF could send over Austria, on a single raid, 187 Lightnings, 50 Thunderbolts, and 48 Mustangs. The P-51 Mustangs belonged to the 31st FG, which was trading its Spitfires for them.

Throughout June the 15th AF brought about an almost complete stoppage of rail traffic in Italy, and on 4 June Allied troops entered Rome. With D-Day in Normandy only two days away, the focus of the Allied war against Germany shifted to France, along with a gradual diminution of Allied strength in Italy. Nevertheless, the Allies remained on the offensive, pushing back the Germans to a new defensive position in the Northern Apennines. The Allies were unable to break out of these mountains into the Po River valley until the following spring, so the war in Italy would extend through another winter.

During the invasion of Southern France that started on 15 August, the 1st and 14th FGs flew strafing missions in direct support, from an airfield in Corsica; while the 82nd FG escorted heavy bombers to the area from Foggia. By the 20th, more than 1,000 sorties were flown, the 14th FG flying 18 missions and the 1st FG flying 21 missions on the first day. During those five days 23 Lightnings were lost.

Above: A 1st FG Lightning touches down on a Corsican airfield during the Southern France Invasion of August 1944. / *Francis J. Pope*

Above: Lightning F-5E-3 (44-23723; modified P-38J-25) of the 23rd PhS, 3rd PhGr, at Florence, Italy, late 1944. / *Roger Besecker*

Right: Lightnings of the 97th FS, 82nd FG, looking for trouble over Northern Italy, late 1944. Black fins/rudders (outside surfaces only), with single digit identifiers, appearing here to be: 'H, O, 6,' and 'W.' / *Edward Jablonski*

Right: Crew Chief Ralph P. Willett with his F-5A-10 (s/n 42-13095), 12th PhS, 3rd PhGr, Florence, Italy, October 1944. Machine was 'gray-white mist' colour, with red prop spinners. *Louise* on left engine nacelle. / *Ralph P. Willett*

Below: Home of the 3rd PhGr, consisting of the 5th, 12th and 23rd PhSs. The 3rd remained in the 12th AF while the P-38 groups transferred to the 15th AF in November 1943. Its sister unit, the 5th PRG, formed in August 1943, shared this field at Florence, but belonged to the 15th AF. / *USAF*

With September came an almost total lack of opposition from the Luftwaffe over Italy. During that month, the 14th FG did not encounter a single enemy aircraft in the course of 18 missions to Yugoslavia, Hungary, Germany, Austria, Czechoslovakia, and Greece. The 82nd FG would claim only four more aerial victories, one of them being a P-51 Mustang!

On 29 October the 82nd flew penetration escort for B-24s to Munich. Before the rendezvous point was reached, a lone P-51B slid into formation with an element of the 95th FS P-38s, at times flying on the wing of Lt Lee Carr. The bombers were picked up and escorted to Munich. After leaving the bombers, most of the 82nd pilots hit the deck to strafe targets of opportunity. When low on ammunition they rejoined, and flew in company with Lt Hawthorn, who had been hit by ground fire and was returning single-engine.

The P-51 reappeared and made several passes on the formation of Lightnings, but each time a P-38 turned into it and it banked away. Finally, it made a straight pass for Lt Hawthorn, guns firing, but Lt Eldon Coulson, with a 45-degree deflection, raked it from nose to cockpit with his .50s and cannon. The Mustang rolled over, went into a spin, and crashed inverted.

Coulson, of course, spent some sleepless nights over the incident until headquarters advised that no P-51s were then assigned to combat operations, and that this one, without drop tanks, was beyond range of any Allied base. Since it was known that the Germans were using at least two Mustangs for this sort of thing, Coulson was credited with a confirmed victory.

Through November, the ground attack missions continued. The P-38s flew escort for the 3rd and 5th photo/recce F-5s into Germany; and when the 82nd FG received a 'Droop Snoot' Lightning, one which had a scaled-down version of a Fortress nose, containing a Norden bombsight, other P-38s temporarily became 'B-38s' for high-level bombing runs led by the 'Droop Snoot'. Just name it; the Lightning could do it.

December offered more of the same, although bomber escort missions were stepped up as the heavys concentrated on oil

Below: Coup de Grace: The 14th FG strikes at the Weiheim marshalling yards in Germany on 19 April 1945. Note P-38 over lower third of the rail yards. / *USAF*

refineries in the Reich, and these targets did provoke fighter opposition.

With the new year came emphasis on strafing and bombing missions in the Northern Apennines Campaign, as the Allies sought to breach the German defences north of the Arno River, where the enemy had dug-in the previous September. During February 1945 the 14th FG alone destroyed more than 100 locomotives in support of this drive. Also in February, four Lightnings of the 49th FS, riding shotgun for an F-5, were bounced by an Me262 jet fighter in the Munich area, and although they were unable to bring their guns to bear on him, they also eluded the jet. The German jets, of course, were too few and too late.

The Allies controlled the air and roamed Germany at will as the heavies continued to pound strategic targets, and the P-38s dropped down to strafe targets of opportunity. The rule for strafing was, 'Low, fast, and once.'

On 24 March the 1st FG formed part of the escort as 15th AF bombers went to Berlin for the first time. Two weeks later, the Allied ground offensive to break out of the Apennines was begun and the P-38s were called upon for direct tactical support. On 11 April 40 Lightnings destroyed 84 locomotives and 43 oil cars and still found time to attack enemy positions in the mountains. But it was dangerous work, and 15 Lightnings were lost with many others damaged on 14 April alone.

On 20 April dive-bombing P-38s cut in 40 places the rail lines leading from the northern entrance to the Brenner Pass, attacked seven rail yards between Innsbruck and Rosenheim, and cut four railway bridges. On the following day, the railway lines between Rosenheim and Munich were accorded similar treatment.

Three days earlier, the US 5th Army broke out of the mountains, crossed the main road west of Bologna, and struck north towards the Po, with the 15th AF wreaking havoc on the roads ahead. Trapped between the 5th Army and the British 8th Army were thousands of Germans. Many more thousands fled northwards, only to be halted by the blown bridges and lack of fuel. On 2 May 1945 nearly a million Germans surrendered, and the war in Italy ended.

From the time the P-38 groups joined the 15th AF, Lightnings were airborne 44,296 times, with 3,814 early returns due to weather or mechanical or other problems, making this airplane 84 per cent effective in combat operations. In 4,004 encounters with enemy aircraft the P-38s destroyed 608, probably destroyed 123, and damaged 343. That results in 15.2 enemy aircraft destroyed per 100 encounters. A total of 131 Lightnings were lost to the enemy, or 3.3 per 100 encounters. The average loss rate was 1.27 per 100 sorties to all causes, flak, enemy aircraft, mechanical, and unknown, while this airplane was operational 75 per cent of the time. A 'sortie' is one plane, one mission. Thus, 40 aircraft on a single mission is recorded as 40 sorties.

The Lightning did not win the war in Italy. However, as in the Pacific, it was *the* fighter-bomber-recce aircraft for that time and place.

Europe

When we look at the Lightning's record in the European Theatre of Operations, the first question that begs an answer is why that record should appear to be, in contrast to P-38 performances elsewhere, somewhat uninspiring. But then, considering the several factors that weighed so heavily against the P-38 groups in England, the second question becomes: How did they ever manage to do so well as they did?

Most, or at least the most vocal P-38 pilots and commanders in England, blamed the airplane for all their troubles, and to a great extent they were right. During the critical, first months of combat operations in the winter of 1943-44, the 20th and 55th FGs were equipped with P-38H models; and although the G and H models had already established outstanding records in the SW Pacific and in the MTO, Lightning pilots in those theatres had seldom had to fight above 30,000ft and had not been forced to fly for long hours at those altitudes at temperatures approaching those prevailing above Europe in wintertime. Therefore, the 8th AF Lightning pilots were the first to face this problem on a daily basis. More than any other single factor, the P-38's lack of adequate windscreen defrosting and cockpit heating (prior to the J models) seriously diminished its effectiveness in the bomber-escort role over Europe. Every ex-Lightning pilot of the 20th and 55th FGs that the authors contacted, voiced this complaint above any other when describing those difficult times. Pilots are human; and when numbed beyond caring by prolonged, intense cold, they are robbed of both judgement and aggressiveness.

That this condition was not corrected via field modification to the aircraft, surely, a reasonably easy task for the Mod Centre at Langford Lodge, appears inexcusable, but no more so, perhaps, than the fact that bolt-on dive flaps, perfected and approved in April 1943, would not be installed on P-38s until June 1944.

The P-38s prior to the J models suffered other major weaknesses at high altitudes. The

supercharger inter-cooler system caused a number of engine failures, especially at the hands of inexperienced pilots. The H model was the first P-38 with automatic engine controls, including automatic oil radiator flaps. Nevertheless, it was still easy to over-boost the engine with a heavy hand on the throttle.

The P-38H models, with 900gal fuel, had a range of 2,000 miles at max cruise and 25,000ft. Maximum speed at 25,000ft was 402mph, and 350mph at 5,000ft. Initial climb rate was 2,800fpm, which was down to 1,700fpm at 25,000ft. Service ceiling was in the vicinity of 40,000ft. Engines were the Allison F-15 series, V-1710-89/91 USAAF designations, normally rated at 1,325hp each, 1,425hp at take-off, and 1,250hp at 25,000ft. These same engines would produce more power at altitude on the J models due to re-design of the inter-cooling system.

There was another factor that surely affected the performance of many P-38 pilots in the 8th AF, and that was low morale through the Winter of 1943-44. In January 1944 Col George Doherty, CO of the 50th FS, arrived in England to form a recce unit, and he recalls this situation: 'I was appalled when I learned that the P-38 fliers in England had an abysmally poor morale because of the high incidence of non-returns suffered by them . . . it seemed to me that the P-38 pilots almost expected each mission to be their last . . .'

When we queried former 20th FG pilot Royal Frey about this, he replied, 'Well,

those Allison "time bombs" didn't help any. That's the term we commonly used when referring to our engines. And there were many cases of frostbite. The lack of adequate cockpit heating went far beyond simple discomfort at those altitudes; it was enervating in the extreme.'

Still, most professional military people will surely agree that morale is largely a matter of proper leadership. During the early, dark days of the war in the Philippines, the abandoned, half-starved, overwhelmingly-outnumbered remnants of the 24th Pursuit Group not only fought with airplanes repaired with bridge timbers and telephone wire, but found a certain humour in the situation, which prompted them to signal: 'Send us another P-40. The one we have is full of holes.'

Contrast that with the attitude of the 8th AF Group Commander who derisively referred to the P-38 as an 'airborne ice-wagon', and something less than a 'real' fighter; or that of the 20th FG Colonel who generously allowed that the P-38 was the 'fifth best fighter in the ETO,' ranking behind the P-51, P-47, Me109, and Fw190. Both of these men had demonstrated unquestioned courage in combat; but their attitudes toward their command responsibilities appear more like that of the man about whom it was said that he was indeed fortunate to have a wife, because he was certain to have problems that could not be blamed on the government.

Marking these several handicaps, perhaps we shall be better equipped to appreciate the courage and devotion to duty that characterised the performances of the Lightning pilots in the ETO.

The first of them to enter combat arrived in England in September 1943, as the 55th FG, consisting of the 38th, 338th, and 343rd FSs. The 55th was based at Nuthampstead, Hertford, and became operational on 15 October with a tentative fighter sweep over Holland. There was no contact with the enemy.

In addition to the 55th FG, the 8th AF Fighter Command at that time contained nine Thunderbolt groups; but the P-47s could range only as far as the German border, leaving the bombers to go it alone into Germany. Therefore, the 55th FG's P-38s, along with those of the 20th FG, which would become operational six weeks later, would have the primary mission of long-range bomber support.

The necessity for such support was shown in dramatic fashion only one day before the 55th began operations, when the US 8th Bomber Command lost 60 Fortresses out of 291 that struck at the ball-bearing works in Schweinfurt.

Long-range bomber escort usually meant that the P-38s would rendezvous with the bombers as the P-47s or Spitfires turned back at the limit of their operating range, and stay with the heavies until other P-47s could pick up the bombers on their way home.

Top left: Lt Gerald A. Brown, 38th FS, 55th FG, accounted for three Me109s and two Fw190s through mid-1944. / *Gerald Brown*

Bottom left: P-38H-5 of the 55th FS, 20th FG, flown by Lt Royal Frey. Frey was shot down 10 February 1944, and spent the rest of the war as a POW. / *Royal Frey*

Below: The 20th FG was initially stationed at Wittering, an RAF station (above); later flew from King's Cliff, Northamptonshire. / *Royal Frey*

An F-5 Lightning buzzes the 91st BG base at Bassingbourn. British light transports on apron appear to be Airspeed Couriers. / *USAF*

The Combined Bomber Offensive against strategic targets deep in Germany had begun in August, and resulted from Allied decisions made at the Casablanca Conference the previous January. Prime Minister Churchill and President Roosevelt had agreed that the RAF, with maximum effort, would raid by night, while the USAAF would do the same by day.

The 55th FG flew three bomber escort missions during October, but encountered almost no enemy air opposition. The 20th FG, based at King's Cliffe, Northampton, received a few P-38s and sent them to fly with the 55th FG, rotating pilots to give each a little experience.

The American contribution to the Combined Bomber Offensive increased slowly if steadily. During November, the 55th FG, usually accompanied by 8-10 Lightnings from the 20th FG (which had received only 16 machines), flew 10 bomber escort missions to Münster, Bremen, Solingen, and targets in Western Germany, as well as strikes against Luftwaffe bases in France. The 55th FG lost 12 Lightnings while claiming 18 enemy aircraft destroyed. The 20th FG lost five and had no claims.

The first big air battle for the P-38s came on 29 November over Bremen when the 55th traded seven P-38s for seven of the enemy. Sixteen Lightnings returned to base with varying degrees of damage. Lt Joe Myers describes his view of that engagement:

'I was flying with my element leader, Lt Gerald Brown, about 10 miles south-west of Bremen on a 210-degree heading at 29,000ft, our flight having been split up due to enemy attacks. I observed a Ju88 approaching the middle box of bombers from the four o'clock position and at bomber level of 26,000ft. We immediately initiated an attack upon him from above and behind. He observed our attack, fired his rockets and dived away to the right. I closed to within about 500 yards, fired a six-second burst, and observed his right engine smoking violently.

'We were losing altitude rapidly, so consequently I broke off the attack and pulled up into a spiralling zoom. As I did so, I observed an Me109 on my wingman's tail about 50 yards behind him. I called him on the R/T, warning him, and advised him to skid until I could position myself for an attack.

'Lt Brown took violent evasive action, doing dives, zooms, skids, rolls, and various other manoeuvres, but the German continued to follow about 50 yards behind, firing continually. In the meantime, I moved to a position about 400 yards behind the Me109, and using full throttle was able to work up on his tail to a position about 150 yards behind him. I had already fired three or four high deflection shots of one or two second's duration at the German, but without noticeable results.

'Finally, Lt Brown tried a skidding barrel roll, but the Messerschmitt followed and put a long burst into Lt Brown's right engine causing heavy, brown smoke to pour out. As the German fired, I fired a five second burst at no-deflection from the inverted position. His engine burst into flames and pieces of the plane flew all over the sky. I passed within 50ft of him and observed fire from the engine streaming back over the fuselage. Lt Brown feathered his right engine and was able to make it back to our home base.'

The 55th FG, with its guests from the 20th FG, tangled with the enemy again on 26 and 29 November as the bombers returned to Bremen, and to Solingen in the Ruhr. On 5 December the bombers went almost 500 miles to Bordeaux, with P-47s providing penetration and withdrawal support, while the 55th FG's P-38s covered the heavies in the target area. No attacks were made on the bombers while under Lightning escort.

Relatively few air battles were fought by the P-38 groups in December, mostly because of the weather, On the 13th they flew a

Above: Lt-Gen Jimmy Doolittle, 8th AF Commander, takes P-38H-5, s/n 42-68972 for a short flight on 23 March 1944. The c/n remains on nose of this one, though it usually gave way to decoration or buzz number. / *USAF*

Left: Lightning F-5 of the 7th Photo Group on the strip at Mount Farm, England. / *USAF*

Above: Lt-Col Cy Wilson led the 55th FS, 20th FG, and became Group Commander 25 June 1944; was shot down to become a POW, and returned to active service with the 20th FG 16 June 1945. / *USAF*

Above left: Decisions, decisions. Top American and British air commanders, General 'Hap' Arnold and Air Chief Marshal Sir Arthur Harris. / *USAF*

Left: Lt-Col Jack Jenkins, 55th FG CO, describes recent air action with typical flyer's gestures to Lt-Col Russ Gustke, Deputy Group Commander, 20th FG. / *USAF*

fighter sweep over France, while the new P-51 Mustangs of the 9th AF's 354th FG flew their first long-range mission, taking the bombers to Kiel.

On 28 December the 20th FG became fully operational, and almost at once began a series of bomber support missions that, during the next 65 days, would range from the Cherbourg Peninsula to Berlin. The 20th FG, it should be noted, was commanded at that time by Col Barton Russell, a fine leader who had little patience with those who derided the P-38. In this he was well supported by Lt-Col Russell Gustke and Maj Frank Clark, formerly of the 14th FG, and veterans of the North African Campaign.

On 29 January Col Russell led the 20th FG as it participated in the biggest raid yet put together by the 8th AF, sending 900 heavies to strike at Frankfurt. Sharing the fighter escort duties were 12 additional fighter groups, including the P-38-equipped 55th FG which would, along with the 20th, and the Mustang-mounted 354th, cover the heavies over the target area.

Approximately 80 enemy single-engine fighters, and 40 twin-engine fighters attempted to attack the bombers; and of the 42 claimed destroyed by the various fighter groups, the 20th FG accounted for 10 and the 55th FG got six. Nine Lightnings were lost, two by collision.

At 11.21hrs as the 20th FG approached its rendezvous with the bombers, just west of the target, the heavies were being attacked. The 20th's 54 Lightnings immediately joined the battle.

Capt Lindol Graham chose an Fw190 on the tail box of bombers, fired a no-deflection burst from the rear, and the enemy exploded. On the way out, near Lille, while covering some cripples, Graham spotted two Fw190s attacking one of them. He closed from 200 yards to 75 yards, giving each a short burst from his cannon and .50s. Both Focke Wulf's exploded and fell in flames. It was later found that Graham expended just 583 rounds of .50-calibre and 36 cannon shells on the three victories.

In the interim, Lts Russell Bond and his wingman Robert Flynn destroyed an Me210 in their crossfire, but then collided and tumbled to earth with their stricken enemy.

While this was happening, Capt Jerome Serros, leading the 55th FS's Yellow Flight, and his wingman, Lt Chester Hallberg, boxed-in an Me110 that was attacking straggling B-24s. The 110 exploded after a four-second burst at very close range and Hallberg flew through the debris.

Meanwhile, Maj Richard Ott flamed an Me110 with a dead astern shot, then shared an Me210 with Lt Walker Whiteside, taking it off the tail of Lt Robert Moss. Maj Ott's left

engine blew at that point and an Me109 immediately fell upon him, but Lt Whiteside sent it down in flames.

Lt Royal Frey in the meantime was pressing home his attack on an Me110, despite accurate return fire from its rear gunner. Frey silenced the gunner, then exploded the 110's fuel tanks, although his P-38 was extensively damaged in the nose and right-engine nacelle.

Assuming that the above-mentioned pilots were typical of 20th FG personnel, we traced their records to learn how they later fared. Lt Frey was shot down less than two weeks later to become a POW. Maj Ott was KIA the very next day. Lt Whiteside was KIA the following August. Capt Graham was KIA in March. Capt Serros was KIA in November 1944; and Lt Hallberg, after 300 combat hours, returned to the US. Clearly, flying a fighter airplane over Hitler's Europe was a job with a very limited future.

But the 8th and 9th Fighter Commands continued the job, of course, and with ever increasing strength. Five additional Lightning groups joined the 8th and 9th AFs during the spring of 1944. In February, the 370th FG was added to the 9th AF, followed by the 474th FG in March and the 367th FG in April. The 8th AF gained the 364th FG in March, and the 479th FG in May. The 7th PhGr had been flying F-5 Lightnings with the 8th AF since the previous November.

Throughout the spring of 1944 the strategic air war against Germany kept the P-38 groups busy with bomber support missions, and meanwhile their effectiveness increased with introduction of the J model Lightnings.

A few P-38J-5s had arrived in England as early as the previous December, although the J-10 and J-15 versions were not in general use until April 1944.

Cockpit heating and windscreen defrosting systems were greatly improved in the J models, and the old circular control wheel was cut-down to a rams-horn type. Externally, the most noticeable change was the deep intakes beneath the propellers which housed core-type radiators, replacing the inter-cooler system previously contained in the wings' leading edges. This arrangement not only gave the pilot direct control over his inter-coolers, eliminating some of the engine-failure causes of the past, but also made room for another 110 gallons of fuel in the wings, which showed up in some J-10s, and all J-15s and subsequent Lightnings. Especially appreciated, was the added power and performance provided by the new inter-cooler system above 25,000ft.

'Big Week' for the American bomber offensive came during a period of good weather, 20-25 February, when more than 1,000 heavy bombers of the 8th AF in England, and 500 heavies of the 15th AF in Italy, blasted German aircraft plants. The 20th and 55th FGs put up an average total of 90 Lightnings for each raid, and though they saw some action, most of the air fighting involved the Thunderbolt groups. An intelligence bulletin records it thus: 'As seems to be his custom, the enemy did not attack the bombers while P-38s were escorting, most probably because 38s can be spotted from great distances . . .'

On 3 March the 20th and 55th FGs went to Berlin for rendezvous with the bombers, but the heavies were recalled because of weather. Therefore, the P-51s had the distinction of flying the first US bomber escort to Berlin on the following day.

A new kind of mission began for the P-38s on 10 April after the Lightning groups received several P-38J-15s converted to 'Droop Snoots' at Langford Lodge. The 'Droop Snoot' idea appears to have originated at Langford Lodge, and William

Above: A P-38J-10 of the 428th FS, 474th FG, 9th AF, skidded off runway into deep mud at Honington. / *USAF*

Left: Early take-off for bomber support mission; 55th FS, 20th FG. / *USAF*

111

Above: Elements of the 383rd FS, 364th FG, 9th AF, which entered combat in April 1944. / *USAF*

Left: D-Day, 6 June 1944, the invasion of Europe. This is how it looked to an F-5 pilot over one of the beachheads. / *USAF*

Above centre: Lt James K. Kunkle of the 401st FS 370th FG, which flew from 'A-1' strip on Omaha Beach in the days following the invasion. / *James Kunkle*

Above right: Capt Vince Hartnett, 434th FS, 479th FG, and his P-38J-15. The 479th suffered high losses due to its large number of strafing missions. / *T. R. Bennett*

Right: Locomotive busting was a high priority task for the Lightnings in the post-invasion period as tactical fighters sought to disrupt enemy supply, communications, and troop movements. / *USAF*

Carter, the military inspector for tooling and assembly there, says he selected 17 aircraft that had been returned from service with combat units for the first conversions. Other 'Droop Snoots' were soon born of field modification in other war theatres, a few reportedly retaining a couple of guns. Some brand new 'Droop Snoots' were eventually produced by the Dallas Modification Centre. Later, the Pathfinder version appeared, containing ground-mapping radar in an elongated nose for bomb-aiming through cloud cover.

The 55th FG flew its first 'Droop Snoot' mission with two squadrons carrying one 1,000lb general purpose bomb and one drop tank on each plane, while the third squadron flew shotgun for them. Led by the 'Droop Snoot' Lightning, the others released their bombs on his signal. Their target was the airfield at St Dizier, but finding it socked-in by weather, the group hit the Coulonniers field instead.

The 20th FG flew a 'Droop Snoot' mission on the same day, taking 26 Lightnings, each with a 1,000lb bomb, to the airdrome at Gütersloh, Germany.

Other 'Droop Snoot' missions followed throughout May and June, the 'B-38s' usually bombing from 20,000ft. After bomb release, they went to the deck to strafe. The Lightnings continued long-range bomber escort as a primary duty, with dive-bombing,

113

Left: Col Ben Kelsey (right) with Col Cass Hough at Honington, 13 September 1944. / *Merle Olmsted*

Right: A 9th AF Lightning at a forward base in Belgium shortly after D-Day. / *USAF*

Below: A P-38H-10 (s/n 42-67987) of the 383rd FS, 364th FG, extensively damaged in wheels-up landing at Honington. / *USAF*

Below right: The 485th FS, 370th FG, carrying 500lb bombs for a dive-bombing attack on Von Rundstedt's tanks and motor transport forces just 15 miles from this airstrip in Belgium. / *USAF*

strafing and 'Droop Snoot' missions filling-in the dates between.

The 474th FG, 9th AF, became operational in April, and Col (ret) Lloyd Wenzel of the 328th FS flew both 'Droop Snoot' and Pathfinder missions:

'We fashioned plywood swaybars wedged on angle-iron affixed to the wing spar, and put belly bands on 2,000lb bombs so we could deliver a 4,000lb load. That load, of course, exceeded the strength of the bomb shackle, which called for low-G manoeuvres and multiple drop (once, only one of mine toggled-off and the recovery G took shackle and all). The plywood sway bars played havoc with the aft boom and horizontal surfaces when the bombs were released, so we finally gave up the 4,000lb loads.

'The 474th was the only P-38 outfit in the ETO at the end of the war. We petitioned General Quesada to let up keep the bird when other groups were changing to P-51s... we had solved the problem of pre-detonation at altitude because of too much cooling in the underslung inter-cooler... we moved the inter-cooler door switch up to the control yoke, and ganged that switch with the gun sight and guns' hot switch so we wouldn't forget to open it.'

Operation Overlord, the invasion of Europe by the Allies, began before dawn on 6 June 1944. D-Day was a Tuesday. Eleven thousand Allied airplanes, painted with special black and white 'invasion stripes' which, it was hoped, would positively identify them to friendly anti-aircraft gunners, flew more than 14,000 sorties over the English Channel, the Normandy beachheads, and beyond into France in support of the landings. On D-Day, and for a week therafter, most of the P-38s were assigned well-defined sections of

airspace above the Channel to protect the mighty shuttle of surface vessels from air attack. The decimated Luftwaffe, however, made few challenges.

Shortly before D-Day, the fourth and last 8th AF Lightning group entered combat as the 479th FG became operational. By 19 June the 479th had lost eight pilots, mostly while strafing in direct support of the Allied troops in Normandy. But bolstered with some veteran 82nd FG pilots such as Clarence Johnson and Ward Kuentzel, the 479th quickly matched the feats of other Lightning groups that were disrupting the enemy's efforts to halt the invading Allied forces.

Throughout June and July, most P-38 missions were flown in support of the heavies which were concentrating on enemy airfields, bridges and railroads. 'Droop Snoot' and strafing missions were sprinkled between, while enemy air opposition continued to dwindle.

If the veteran 20th and 55th FGs had found their opportunities for shooting down significant numbers of German aircraft quite limited, the Lightning groups that followed them into combat found their chances almost non-existent. The day-to-day intelligence summaries of missions, flown by the P-38 groups end, with monotonous repetition: 'There were no attacks on the bombers while under P-38 escort,' or 'no ea sighted.'

This had been largely true even during late 1943 and early 1944, when the Thunderbolt groups were fighting large-scale air battles almost daily. The most common explanation for this situation was that the German fighters were ordered to avoid combat with all Allied fighters if possible, and concentrate on the bombers. Since the P-38s were easily recognised, even at great distances, the enemy simply attacked the bomber stream at other points.

Top left: Allied fighters took over Luftwaffe fields on the Continent as the enemy retreated. In foreground, 485th FS Lightning, and in background machines of the 402nd FS, 370th FG. / *USAF*

Centre left: A Lightning J-10 model of the 429th FS, 474th FG, returns from a mission with one engine out. / *USAF*

Bottom left: Maj R. C. 'Buck' Rogers of the 367th FG, in France, 12 October 1944. / *USAF*

Right: This view of a new P-38H-5 showing gun-camera position which resulted in blurred pictures and many unconfirmed victories. Camera was switched to the left under-wing pylon on L models. / *Edward Jablonski*

Below: P-38L-1 of the 429th FS, 474th FG is serviced on a grey winter's day at Ophoven, Belgium. / *USAF*

There were, of course, far more Thunderbolts than Lightnings in the ETO, a total of 22 P-47 groups in the 8th and 9th AFs, as opposed to seven P-38 groups, and most of the Thunderbolt groups were there before the first P-38 arrived.

Actually, the P-38's history in the ETO is a relatively short one (except for that of the 474th FG), because soon after General Jimmy Doolittle assumed command of the 8th AF, he decided, in the spring of 1944, to replace all P-38s and P-47s with the new P-51 as soon as possible. He could hardly go wrong, because the Merlin-powered Mustang was an excellent fighter aircraft. The only question one might raise is: was it really needed? After all, the rugged, battle-proven P-47 'Jug' had already broken the back of the Luftwaffe in aerial combat; and the first truly combat-ready Lightning, the P-38J-25, would be entering service in August. Doolittle may well have been influenced, however, by the numerous complaints against the P-38G and early J models that accumulated during the

winter; plus the fact that General Kenney in the SW Pacific, and General Twining in Italy were clamouring for all the P-38s they could get.

The 20th and 55th FGs transitioned to Mustangs in July 1944. The 479th and 364th began receiving P-51s in mid-September. By the end of January 1945, the 9th AF Lightning groups had been similarly re-mounted, except for the 367th, which traded its P-38s for P-47s, and the 474th FG which pleaded successfully to keep its P-38s. The 474th was the only P-38 FG in the ETO when Germany surrendered in May 1945.

While flying P-38s, the 20th FG destroyed 89 German aircraft in air combat, and lost 79 pilots, 46 KIA, and 55 POWs. The 20th dropped 600,000lb of bombs, and shot-up numberless locomotives and other ground targets. The 55th FG established a similar record. Other P-38 groups in the ETO claimed fewer enemy aircraft destroyed in the air, but greater destruction against ground targets.

Left: Plotting Section of the 33rd PRS prepares photos for the photo interpreters. / *Sterling Winn*

Below: Lightning F-5B-1s of the 34th PhS, Exchwege, Germany, April 1945. German prisoners marching in background. / *USAF*

Far East Victory 1944-1945

The Allied drive to the Philippines was a giant encircling manoeuvre, consisting of a series of amphibious operations by three Allied forces, beneath skies controlled by Allied fighters. The US Navy and Marines, with the US 7th AF, swept across the Central Pacific to occupy islands in the Gilberts, Marshalls, and Marianas to close off the northern and eastern segments of the circle. Another US Navy and Marine force, along with the 13th AF, fought through the Solomons to seal the southern segment, while MacArthur's army forces, US, Australian, and New Zealanders, with the US 5th AF overhead, swept northward to the Admiralties and the length of the New Guinea to Morotai, closing the western segment of the ring. The Japanese strongholds at Rabaul on New Britain, and Truk in the Carolines, were in the centre, denied reinforcements, supplies, or the chance to escape. The enemy's attempts at all three proved exceedingly costly in ships, men, and aircraft.

MacArthur's forces seized Morotai, just 275 miles from the southern tip of the Philippines, on 15 September 1944, and on the same day Nimitz sent the US 1st Marine Division ashore on Peleliu in the southern Palaus, 500 miles to the north-east of MacArthur. In seven months MacArthur's forces had driven nearly 1,500 miles from the Admiralties to Morotai; in 10 months Nimitz's forces had advanced more than 4,500 miles from Hawaii to the Palaus. From these hard-won bases, the invasion of the Philippines would be launched a month later.

During those 10 months, there were some changes in P-38 strength in the SW Pacific. In December 1943 the 9th FS 49th FG, and the 39th FS 35th FG, which were discussed earlier, had their Lightnings taken from them to provide replacement aircraft for the 475th FG. The 49th and 35th FGs were then completely re-equipped with P-47 Thunderbolts, a circumstance that occasioned a chorus of anguished cries from the pilots of the 9th and 39th Squadrons.

Therefore, during the early months of 1944, the 5th AF contained but one P-38 group, the 475th, which operated with its own three squadrons (431st, 432nd, and 433rd), plus the Lightning-equipped 80th FS from the 8th FG.

Then, in April 1944, the 8th FG's two remaining squadrons (35th and 36th) were equipped with P-38s to make two full-strength Lightning groups in the 5th AF.

Below: Capt Warren R. Lewis' machine at Strip 3, Nadzab, in the Markham Valley, New Guinea, March 1944. This was one of the first unpainted J models to reach the 475th FG. / *Carroll R. Anderson*

Left: A 475th FG Lightning over the Markham Valley, New Guinea. Ever-present grass fires in the valley made the airstrips easy to find. / *Steve Birdsall via Bruce Hoy*

Below left: Charles A. Lindbergh (left) and Thomas B. McGuire, Jr, Hollandia, June 1944. Mr Lindbergh showed P-38 pilots how to increase range of their machines with proper engine settings, a technique long known to veteran pilots, but not taught by Army flying schools. With proper fuel management, carrying 1,000gal of petrol, P-38Js and Ls could remain aloft for up to 12 hours, flying as far as 2,500 miles. / *Carroll R. Anderson*

Below: Dick Bong with another of his several P-38s. His fiancée's picture tore away in flight shortly after this photo was made in April 1944, at either Nadzab or Gusap, New Guinea. / *Carl Bong*

123

Above: The P-38L assigned to Capt John A. Tilley, 431st FS, 475th FG, Philippines, early 1945.
/ *John A. Tilley*

Left: Along with improved engines and other changes, the L model Lightning had gun camera mounted on left under-wing pylon to eliminate blurred pictures resulting from guns' vibration.
/ *Lockheed California Company*

Top right: Tube-type rocket launchers tried on P-38s were not successful. The 'Christmas-tree' type worked well, and fittings for it were added to production L models. It was also field-retro-fitted to some earlier Lightnings.
/ *Mitch Mayborn*

Right: Dive flaps, which largely eased the Lightning's compressibility problem, are seen extended beneath the wings of this P-38L-5, c/n 8483. / *Edward Jablonski*

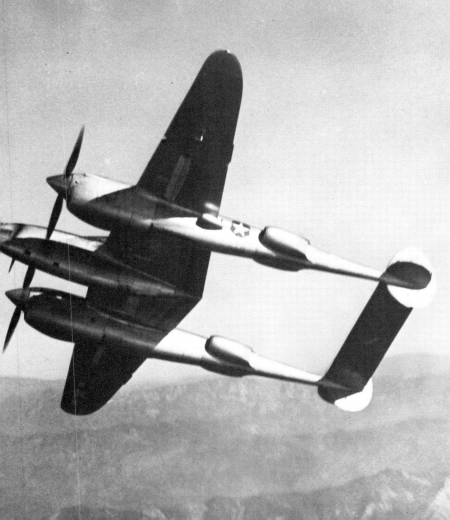

A month later, the 9th FS 49th FG, received new P-38J-15s, while the 7th and 8th FSs continued with P-47s until September, when the entire group was given new P-38J-25s.

Meanwhile, in August, the 18th FG of the 13th AF, a veteran P-40 outfit that had fought in the Solomons, was equipped with new P-38s and transferred, along with the 347th FG, to New Guinea for the coming assault on the Philippines.

The 5th AF, now commanded by Lt-Gen Ennis Whitehead, and the 13th AF, under Maj-Gen St Clair Street, were meanwhile placed in the new Far East Air Forces (FEAF) with General Kenney commanding.

So, at last, General Kenney would be fat with P-38s, approximately 500 of them, including those of the 6th PrG (5th AF), and the 4th PhG (13th AF) and he was pleased.

His pilots were pleased, too, and Carroll Anderson remembers:

'... the feeling of exultation as we sped lower and lower at Dobo coming home from a mission; 16 P-38s, wingtip to wingtip, as tight as we could get, with Warren Lewis bringing us so low we barely cleared the little valley where we were quartered. All four flights would be locked as close as possible, because Lewis wanted everyone to know that

Possum Squadron flew the best formation in the group, and we damned well did.'

'Possum' Squadron was the 433rd FS of the 475th FG. The 475th moved up to Noemfoor Island, off the north-east coast of Dutch New Guinea, prior to the seizure of Morotai. During this period, the 475th contained two of the seven Lightning pilots in the theatre who would down 20 or more enemy aircraft, at least three of which developed a visible rivalry for the title of top American ace. These were Maj Richard I. Bong, Maj Thomas B. McGuire, and Lt-Col Thomas J. Lynch.

Bong was a 'nice guy' type, sincere and full of youthful enthusiasm. McGuire was the opposite, an intense, demanding man who seemed forever disappointed at the imperfections of his fellows. He was not generally liked. Lynch was an outstanding fighter leader and disciplinarian, a professional soldier who led by example, and was much respected by his men.

Bong was clearly favoured by General Kenney (which was probably as great an injustice to Bong as anyone else), and was allowed such latitude of action, without command obligations, that he was, in effect, a free agent. McGuire, who had flown P-39s in the Aleutians early in the war, came to the 49th FG for a brief time, then transferred to the 475th FG, taking command of the 431st FS in May 1944. Lynch led the 39th FS, and had shot down three enemy fighters while flying P-39s, an impressive record in itself.

Above: Revetments of the 9th FS,
49th FG, Tacloban, Leyte, late 1944.
Gerald Johnson, taxying, would
eventually have 24 aerial victories.
/ *George Walker via Carl Bong*

Top left: On the eve of the Iwo Jima
Campaign, the veteran 28th PhS
photographed enemy positions from
altitudes as low as 50ft. This 28th
PhS F-5B-1 on Saipan, 10 July 1944,
has the early, curved windscreen of
the P-38J-5, although this batch of
F-5B-1s was built concurrent with
the P-38J-10s. / *USAF*

Left: Col Robert E. Westbrook,
leading ace of the 13th AF with 20
aerial victories, was killed on
22 November 1944, while leading
the 18th FG in a strafing attack on
enemy shipping. Westbrook was on
the first mission of his eighth
combat tour. / *USAF*

Right: In mid-November 1944, the
Thunderbolt-equipped 318th FG,
7th AF, received 30 Lightnings
which they formed into the
'Lightning Provisional Group' for
long-range support of 20th AF
bombers. Above is a 318th Jug,
P-38, and a 47th FS (15th FG)
Mustang over Saipan. / *USAF*

127

The so-called 'race of aces' in the SW Pacific appears to have begun in February 1944; and at that time included Maj Neel Kearby, 340th FS 348th FG, who ferverently believed in the superiority of the 340th's P-47 Thunderbolts. But Kearby was shot down on 4 March 1944, at which time he had 25 victories.

Just four days later, Col Lynch was killed by return fire from enemy shipping during a strafing run. He had 21 victories at the time. McGuire had 16, and Bong 24.

Enemy aircraft were rarely encountered throughout the summer, and by 1 October, on the eve of the Philippine invasion, McGuire's score stood at 21, Bong's at 28.

Then, while the 6th PhR group was earning a Distinguished Unit Citation mapping the Leyte area in the Central Philippines, the rest of the FEAF was striking at the enemy's oil facilities at Balikpapan, Borneo, 800 miles west of Noemfoor, and Japanese fighters rose in strength once again to defend that vital installation.

On 10 October, Bong, officially attached to 5th AF Headquarters, flew with the 49th FG as they covered 58 Liberators over Balikpapan, and destroyed two enemy planes, an Oscar and a 'Nick' (Kawasaki Ki-45, Type 2, twin-engine fighter).

Four days later McGuire, uninvited, tagged along with the 49th to the same target where 50 enemy fighters were waiting. He shot down three of them, an Oscar, 'Hamp' (same as Zeke or Zero-Sen), and 'Tojo' (Nakajima Ki-44, Type 2, similar to Oscar).

About the middle of the month, the first P-38L models arrived in the SW Pacific, and while these airplanes were fitted with V-1710-111/113 engines that would deliver 1,600hp (war emergency) some 2,000ft higher than before, this advantage was largely off-set by a 500lb increase in aircraft weight. The gadgeteers had got some of their 'gizmos' and 'whatchamacallits' installed to complicate and add weight; pressurised drop tanks, and a tail-mounted mini-radar to warn of attack from the rear, for example, and though the L models should not be described as inferior to the J-25s, much of their superiority was on paper. The improved supercharger controls simply did not make all that much difference, particularly since enemy air opposition, in all theatres, had dwindled to a small fraction of that faced by P-38 pilots a year earlier.

With two 300gal drop tanks, the L model had a range of 2,600 miles at economy cruise above 10,000ft. Maximum speeds were about the same as those of the J-25 model, 415mph, for example, at 18,000ft. Carrying external ordnance of 3,200lb the Ls had a radius of action of about 450 miles.

Externally, the L models were quickly identified by the landing light mounted flush in the leading edge of the left wing, perhaps a tip-off, along with the extra range, of Lockheed's hopes of extending P-38 production with the P-38M Night Lightning. (In November 1944 two P-38Js were painted black, given APS-4 radar, and tested over Leyte by the 547th NFS.)

Left: Lightning F-5 *Frantic*, 8th PrG, gives up its film upon return to base at Ling Ling, China, after flying 1,600 miles to Yawata, Japan and return. / *USAF*

Below: Capt William Beardsley and T/Sgt V. DeVito add mission symbol to the *Golden Eagle*, a 449th P-38G-10 that had previously served in North Africa. / *USAF*

The campaign for the Philippines began on 20 October when MacArthur's American and Australian forces landed at Tacloban and Dulag on Leyte Gulf. The airstrip at Tacloban was ready just after noon on the 27th, and as the last steel mat was put down on the 2,800ft landing surface, the 49th FG arrived with 34 Lightnings, the first American aircraft on Philippine soil since May 1942. Bong was among them.

That afternoon, five Japanese fighters approached the field and some 49th FG 'rank' went up to intercept. Lt-Col Bob Morrisey, Lt-Col Gerald Johnson (14 victories at the time; 24 eventually), Lt-Col George Walker, and Maj Bong. Johnson got two, leaving Morrisey and Bong to destroy one each. The next day, Bong got two more.

The Tacloban-Dulag area fast became swollen with aircraft as General Kenney moved in his air groups for the extended offensive up the Philippines. The 475th FG joined the 49th to operate out of Leyte and John Tilley (five official victories) remembers that field:

'When my squadron, the 431st, first arrived at Leyte on 30 October, we operated out of a mud field which was about 2,800ft from palm tree to palm tree. For take-off, Cletracs would tow us from the dispersal area and back our booms into the palm trees at one end of the field. The brakes wouldn't hold in the mud, so as soon as we got the engines started we'd cram on full throttle and go. No mag checks; just fire up and go. About half

way down the field we'd slap down half flaps, haul back on the yoke, and pray. To my constant surprise, I'd always clear the palm trees at the far end.

'For landing, the flaps were full-down, the props flat, and oil and coolant radiator doors full-open for additional drag. I'd have opened the side window and stuck out my hand for even more drag if both hands hadn't been busy. We'd then bring it in as slow as possible, barely clearing the tops of the trees, and drop it into the mud with a splash that covered the whole damned plane. When we stopped sliding we'd cut the engines and the Cletrac would tow us out of the way so the next intrepid birdman could splash down.'

For six weeks following the invasion, the Japanese sent a series of convoys to reinforce their positions in the Leyte area. The weather was bad, there was bitter fighting on land, and three great sea battles, collectively known as the Battle of Leyte Gulf, were fought. The 49th and 475th FGs bombed and strafed in support of the Allies' tenuous presence on Leyte. On the 2nd, the 49th downed 26 enemy aircraft, while the 8th and 347th FGs claimed 75 destroyed on the

ground at Bacolod, Carolina, Alicante, and Cebu. One of the Japanese pilots killed over Leyte at that time was Lt Goro Furugori, who had more than 30 victories, two of them were P-38s.

Also during these battles, the 13th AF's ranking ace, Lt-Col Robert B. Westbrook, brought his total socre to 20 aerial victories, 13 of which were counted in P-38s. He was killed on 22 November while flying with the 18th FG.

On 10 November every available P-38 was up to strike at another Japanese convoy approaching Ormoc, a few miles south of Tacloban on Leyte. Lt Chris Herman of the 431st FS recalled that 'Our CO (McGuire) knocked off two more for a total of 26 . . . the CO got nicked too; part of a Nip plane he shot up tore off the top of his canopy and creased his noggin. Later, he got an engine shot out while strafing a troop convoy.'

Most of the Lightnings were committed to the Philippines, although the 347th FG was given the task of hitting the enemy's air and shipping buildup in the Makassar area of the Celebes from a base on Middleburg Island. Flying missions on 7, 20, and 22 November, the group received a Distinguished Unit

Above: Pilots of the 9th PRS with an F-5E-2 converted from a P-38J-15, Dum Dum, India. And a pox on the AAF photographer for not listing the names of these men! / *USAF*

Top left: Lt Harry H. Sealy of the 459th 'Twin Dragons,' Upper Assam, India, early 1944. / *William Broadfoot*

Bottom left: Tube-type launcher for 4.5in M-8 rockets is installed on P-38J-5 of the 459th FS which was based at Chittagong on the Bay of Bengal from 4 March 1944 to the end of December 1944. / *USAF*

Citation for pressing home their attacks in the face of intense enemy opposition. The 347th also struck at the oil refineries at Tarakan, Borneo, to strafe and bomb with incendiaries.

The anniversary of the Pearl Harbor attack was to be the date of the major engagement to secure Leyte. Lightnings, Thunderbolts, Warhawks, and Navy Corsairs covered the amphibious assault at Ormoc on 7 December 1944. While some carried bombs to support the landings, Lightnings of the 49th and 475th FGs took care of enemy air opposition. All were so effective that Admiral Kinkaid characterised the action as the finest air support that he had seen in the SW Pacific. Lt-Col Charles H. MacDonald led the 475th on four missions over the beaches, shooting down three enemy aircraft to bring his score to 22 (ultimately 28); and Lt-Col Gerald R. Johnson of the 49th FG also got three of the 53 Japanese fighters claimed that day.

Gerald (no one ever called him 'Jerry') Johnson would later gain a total of 24 air victories and survive the war only to sacrifice his life to save that of a fellow passenger who had no parachute in a stricken transport plane. Johnson gave the man his own parachute, then went down with the aircraft.

Gerald Johnson had flown P-39s in the Aleutians before coming to the 49th FG in the SW Pacific; and he has been characterised as 'ruthless' by some, but that is hard to reconcile with an incident that took place over New Guinea late in 1943. He and James 'Duck-Butt' Watkins were part of a 49th FG rout of a Japanese fighter formation, and one of the few remaining enemy pilots was fighting fiercely for his survival. Surrounded by American fighters and ripped by numerous hits, the gutsy Japanese refused to quit and, in fact, was getting in some telling blows himself. The Americans finally gave up the chase as the enemy fighter circled just off the water waiting for the next attack. At that point, Gerald Johnson dived upon him, then banked away, waggling his wings in salute. The Japanese returned the gesture, then flew away.

On the 17th, Bong got his 40th official victory, an Oscar, over San Jose, and General Kenney sent him back to the US to stay. He was killed 6 August 1945, flying a P-80 jet fighter.

On Christmas Day, as the campaign against Manila began with raids on Clark Field, Tom McGuire downed three enemy fighters, following up the next day with four more. That brought McGuire's total to 38, and General Kenney promptly grounded him until Bong could be properly honoured back home. McGuire was flying again on 7 January, but while engaged with an enemy fighter at very low altitude stalled his P-38 in

a tight turn and crashed to his death. The 'race of aces' was over.

Although Japanese troops in Leyte's north-western mountains would hold out well into the spring of 1945, MacArthur moved on to Luzon, putting ashore four army divisions in Lingayen Gulf on 9 January 1945. Three days later, this force was driving across the Central Plains of Luzon toward Manila.

Meanwhile, two 'orphan' squadrons of P-38s were fighting in Burma and China, the 449th and 459th FSs. The 449th was formed in July 1943, with pilots in North Africa who volunteered to fly their planes to China. The 459th FS was activated two months later as the 4th Squadron of the Warhawk-equipped 80th FG which was based in Upper Assam, India.

The Kunming-based 449th FS belonged to Brig-Gen Claire Chennault's 14th AF, and shared missions with the 23rd FG, the latter having taken over the planes and duties of the famed Flying Tigers the previous July.

From Kunming, and later from Ling-Ling, the 449th, led by Maj Ed Goss and Capt Sam Palmer, produced several aces; but enemy air opposition was sporadic, and the squadron expended most of its efforts against enemy supply lines. Lt Tom Harmon, a famous football player (and nowadays a TV sportscaster) flew with the 449th. In an air battle over Klukiang, Harmon was shot down, but despite painful burns managed to

Above: Capt Walter F. Duke of the 459th FS 'Twin Dragons' scored 13 aerial victories in the China-Burma-India Theatre. / *William Broadfoot*

Top left: Bombing-up a 459th FS P-38J-10 at Chittagong, December 1944. / *USAF*

Bottom left: Miss Virginia E, an F-5B-1 of the 9th PRS, leaves revetment area at Rumkhapalong on the India-Burma Border. / *USAF*

133

walk back to his home field, a journey requiring 32 days.

The 459th FS, which became well-known in the China-Burma-India Theatre (CBI) as the 'Twin Dragons', was commanded by Maj John E. Fouts and Capt Verl Luchring. As part of the 80th FG, it belonged to General Lewis Brereton's 10th AF, and its primary mission was to protect the terminals in India and the Air Transport Command cargo planes that flew over the Himalayas to China supplying Chiang Kai-shek and the 14th AF. The 459th also supported Allied ground operations in northern Burma as Chinese troops under General Stilwell slowly regained that land, with guerilla outfits led by British General Orde Wingate and US General Frank Merrill ('Merrill's Marauders') harassing the enemy's flanks.

On 4 March 1944 the Twin Dragons moved to Chittagong on the Bay of Bengal, attached to RAF 224 Group, and between 11 March and 26 May destroyed 123 enemy aircraft. Then, as evidence of the rapidly dwindling strength of the Japanese Air Force, the 459th could add but 29 additional victories throughout the next 11 months.

The Twin Dragons did, however, become expert bridge busters. They moved to Rumkhapalong on the India-Burma border in January 1945 and during one nine-day period, destroyed 11 rail and road bridges. A week later, they knocked out three more in a single day.

Capt Walter F. Duke was the Dragon with the fieriest breath, scoring 10 confirmed air victories before he went down over Burma.

Maj Maxwell H. Glenn had a total of eight, five of them in one day. Major Hampton E. Boggs scored nine kills in the air, and several other 459th pilots could count five apiece.

The makeshift war in China gradually slowed during 1945 after the Allies decided against landings on the China Coast, opting instead to take Iwo Jima in the Bonin Islands, and Okinawa in the Ryukyus. With these as air and naval bases at Japan's very doorstep, the final assault, and its subsequent supply, would much resemble that which was visited upon Hitler's Europe the year before.

In the meantime, another P-38 unit was formed. It appeared much too late to claim significant numbers of enemy aircraft shot down, but it did see some action, and served as a comforting 'security blanket' for some bomber crews. This unit was born in mid November 1944 when the 318th FG 7th AF, equipped with P-47 Thunderbolts, was assigned to support 20th AF bombers operating from Saipan in the Marianas. The P-47s hardly possessed sufficient range (and their pilots were undoubtedly a mite uncomfortable with one engine over all that water), so 30 Lightnings were sent to the 318th, spread among its three squadrons (19th, 33rd, and 73rd) and, after four or five hours' practice, the 'Jug' drivers bounded off in their new P-38s, with 26 Liberators, to raid Truk.

Over the target, only one floatplane came up to intercept the bombers, so the P-38s went down to deal with some Zekes that were harassing an American convoy. Maj

D. Jack Williams, 19th FS CO, blew the tail off one enemy fighter with four short bursts. Lt Boone Ruff overtook another and flamed it, then Maj John Hussey was surprised at the destructive power of his 20mm as he fired a single burst which tore the left wing from a third Zeke. Two more Zekes went down before the guns of other 318th pilots.

A few days later, the group's P-38s were formed into the Lightning Provisional Group, 20th AF, and during December they flew more than 500 combat hours, including three missions to Iwo Jima and one to Truk, averaging 1,500 miles each time.

On 5 January 1945 the Provisional Lightnings took the Liberators to Iwo Jima again. It was an uneventful mission for all but Lt Fred Erbele. Strafing enemy gun positions, he caught a 20mm round which tore off the spinner and destroyed propeller control of his left engine. Another round left his right wing burning and knocked-out aileron control. With airspeed down to 150mph he managed to restart the left engine and climbed to 5,000ft before it overheated. The flames were out but there was an enormous hole in the right wing near the trailing edge.

Erbele attempted to form-up with the other P-38s, but his left prop could not be feathered and the resultant drag held him down to 135mph. The group could not afford to stay with him, but two Liberators dropped their flaps, tucked-in on each side, and indicated that they would see him home.

The windmilling propeller set up extreme vibration throughout the aircraft and wreaked havoc with the instrument panel. It

Above: This early F-4 Lightning was flown by the Royal Australian Air Force No 1 Photo Reconnaissance Unit. / *Frank F. Smith*

Top left: A P-38 of the 449th FS is inspected by Chinese troops on the 23rd FG (P-40s) field at Kunming, China. / *USAF*

Centre left: An 18th FG machine on Palawan in 1945. The 18th and 347th FGs of the 13th AF flew long-range missions to Borneo in addition to fighting the Philippine Campaign. / *Frank F. Smith*

Bottom left: An F-5 Lightning of the 28th PhS on Iwo Jima, March 1945. / *USAF*

This 28th PhS F-5E (converted P-38J-20) has an escort of Marine Corsairs because Marine 1-Lt David D. Duncan is squeezed into the modified drop tank to identify and photograph enemy positions on Okinawa, from altitudes as low as 100ft. / *Mitch Mayborn*

423280

Left: P-38L-5s of the 6th AF guarding the Panama Canal, December 1944. / *USAF*

Right: Charles Lindbergh taxis for take-off in the machine of Lt-Col Meryl Smith, Deputy Group Commander of the 475th FG. On 28 July 1944, Lindbergh shot down a Mitsubishi Ki-51 *Sonia*, but the victory is not included in the 475th's total of 545 enemy aircraft downed during its two years in combat. / *Carroll R. Anderson*

occurred to Erbele that anything that was not fastened very securely was certain to come unstuck, including any possible fillings in his teeth. His canopy had also been shot away, but that didn't matter much, until they encountered a storm front.

Somehow Erbele managed to keep the crippled Lightning reasonably upright through the turbulence and emerged from the storm wet but still flying. Then a couple of Thunderbolts picked him up and led him to Saipan where he landed with 20 minutes' fuel remaining after flying his bucking bronco for 4hr 20min.

We relate the above not because it is an unusual story, but rather because it is typical. A thousand other P-38 pilots in World War II brought their Lightnings home in similar, or worse, conditions.

This provokes the telling of an alleged incident that took place during the battle for Manila. A P-38 pilot from the 49th FS heard someone call in distress. 'My engines hit! I'm losing coolant! What shall I do?' To which the 49'er responded, 'Calm down and feather it.' Came the dejected reply, 'Feather, hell, I'm flying a Mustang!'

On the eve of the assault upon Iwo Jima, Lightnings of the 28th Phr Squadron, led by Capt Edward S. Taylor, flew within 50ft of the enemy positions to get their pictures. Ground fire was intense, so 12 P-38s flew line-abreast with two F-5s, as the photo craft, flown by Capt Bennie Bearden and Lt Don Howard, made three passes to map the entire island.

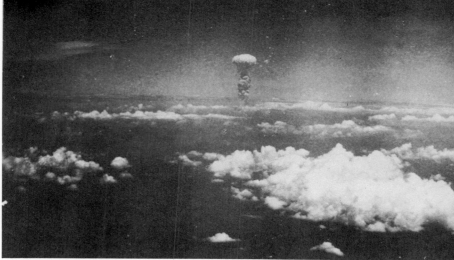

Two US Marine divisions fought their way ashore at Iwo Jima on 19 January 1945 and the Provisional Lightnings of the 318th FG were overhead that day, and for days afterwards, while one of the bloodiest ground battles of the war was slowly resolved. Not until the end of March was a fighter strip ready for use on Iwo. Then 7th Fighter Command moved in, a bit prematurely, as it turned out.

On the night of 27 March, after the Marines had moved out and before Army troops arrived to replace them, Japanese hold-outs on the island mounted a 'banzai' attack on the airstrip, and 7th AF personnel fought hand-to-hand with the enemy in the darkness. The airmen, however, proved to be pretty good combat infantrymen. Seventh Fighter Command lost 44 officers and men killed, 88 wounded, while the bodies of 333 enemy soldiers were found when morning came.

American forces invaded Okinawa on 1 April, and neighbouring Ie Shima was occupied on the 16th. The enemy, however, was so solidly entrenched in *Shuri* positions, a maze of tunnels and caves, on Okinawa, that the island was not secured until 21 June.

Right: On 19 August 1945, the Japanese surrender envoys are led into Ie Shima by a B-25 Mitchell of the 499th BS, 345th BG. A B-17 carrying a lifeboat flies alongside, and P-38s of the 49th FG circle overhead. / *USAF*

Centre left: On 6 August 1945, Charles Lerable had been over Japan in his F-5 Lightning on a photo mission when he saw an unusual 'thunder-head' in the distance. He photographed it and unwittingly got a candid shot of the Hiroshima A-bomb cloud.

Bottom left: Col George 'Raven' Laven, 7th FS, 49th FG, and *Itsy Bitsy II*, a P-38L-5. A previous *Itsy Bitsy* was a P-38E that Laven flew in the Aleutians three years earlier. On 21 June 1945, Laven scored the last of the 49th's 678 aerial victories in World War II. / *George Laven*

Above: Guy Watson, 8th FS, 49th FG, and his P-38L *Sacca Mauree.*
/ Guy Watson

Centre right: Three red stripes on aft booms identify this P-38L as the craft of Col George Walker, 49th FG Group Commander. Red spinners indicate that Walker flew with the 9th FS. Photo taken at Tacloban, late 1944.
/ George Walker via Carl Bong

Bottom right: Biak, 10 October 1944; just returned from mission to the Balikpapan oil refineries are (left to right) Col George Walker, 49th FG CO, Maj Wallace Jordan, 9th FS CO, Maj Richard Bong, and Lt-Col Gerald Johnson, Deputy Group CO, 49th FG.
/ George Walker via Carl Bong

Manila had been liberated four months earlier, and by 28 June most 5th AF units moved up to bases on Okinawa and Ie Shima to join the 7th and 20th AFs who were there for the assault on the Japanese home islands. Early in May, American fighters from Okinawa were ranging over Japan.

Enemy air opposition was almost non-existent during the last months of the Pacific war, and it seems nearly impossible to determine just who shot down the last Japanese airplane. A P-61 Black Widow night fighter of the 458th NFS claimed an Oscar on 14 August, the day Japan sued for peace.

The Lightnings, of course, ranged far and wide looking for prey until the very end, but the only targets they could find were on the surface. Maj (later Col) George Laven scored the last aerial victory for the 49th FG.

Laven, who flew P-38s in the Aleutians early in the war, was looking for trouble over Formosa on 21 June 1945 when he found and destroyed an 'Emily' (Kawanishi H8K1-2, four-engine flying boat). Since it was Laven's fifth confirmed kill, it also made him the last P-38 ace.

We mark Col Laven's record not only for his five aerial victories, but also for the 60,000 tons of enemy shipping and 69 locomotives he destroyed while bombing and strafing; and for the 59 times he returned to base on one engine during three years of combat.

Somehow, these few facts, taken from the service record of a single P-38 pilot, seem to sum up effectively all that we have tried to report here about the Lightning and the men who flew her.

Below: The pioneering 8th PhS, originally led by Karl Polifka, moved to Motabu Airstrip on Okinawa in June 1945. By then, the eight-ball had become its official squadron insignia. / *USAF*

P-38 Production

The following list was compiled from USAAF, Lockheed, and US Department of Commerce records, the latter providing a month-by-month production break-down, along with aircraft delivery dates.

Lockheed produced a total of 9,923 P-38s, plus the XP-49, which was assembled from P-38 spares. An additional 113 P-38s were built at Nashville, Tennessee, by Consolidated Vultee, making a total of 10,036 machines in all. Aircraft quantities shown in parentheses indicate airplanes converted at the Dallas Modification Centre, Texas. Another mod centre operated in Australia, and a third at Langford Lodge, near Belfast.

The USAAF serial numbers (s/n) were cross-checked from the several available sources, including the individual aircraft record cards. The builder's or constructor's serial numbers (c/n), however, do not admit to much sceptical examination since these come from a single source. But we were pleased (and a little surprised) to find that the totals obtained from each source were in agreement.

The careful researcher will note that c/n's in the 7101/7900 range were employed twice by Lockheed, although the prefixes, '222', and '422', indicating Lockheed model designations, are different.

AF Model	Quantity	USAAF Serial	Lockheed Serial	Delivery Date
XP-38	1	37-457	22-2201	2/39
YP-38	13	39-689/701	122-2202/2214	9/40 thru 5/41
P-38	29	40-744/761	222-2215/2232	6/41 into 8/41
		763/773		
XP-38A	1	762	622-2233	8/41
P-38D	36	774/809	222-2245/2280	8/41 into 10/41
P-38E	210	41-1983/2097	5201/5315	10/41 into 2/42
		2100/2110	5318/5338	
		2172,	5390,	
		2219,	5437,	
		2221/2292	5439/5510	
F-4-1 (P-38E)	99	2098/2099	5316/5317	10/41 into 2/42
		2121/2156	5339/5374	
		2158/2171	5376/5389	
		2173/2218	5391/5436	
		2220	5438	
F-5A-2 (P-38E)	1	2157	5375	1/42
P-322	143	RAF s/n AE 978 thru AF 220		2/42 into 4/42
P-38F	128	41-2293/2321	222-5511/5539	3/42 into 5/42
		2323/2358	5541/5576	
		2382/2386	5600/5604	
		2388/2392	5606/5610	
		7486/7496	5613/5623	
		7498/7513	5625/5640	
		7516/7524	5643/5651	
		7526/7530	5653/5657	
		7532/7534	5659/5661	
		7536/7538	5663/5665	
		7542/7543	5669/5670	
		7545/7547	5672/5674	
		7551	5678	

AF Model	Quantity	USAAF Serial	Lockheed Serial	Delivery Date
F-4A-1 (P-38F)	20	2362/2381	5580/5599	3/42
P-38F-1	148	2322	5540	5/42 into 6/42
		2359/2361	5577/5579	
		2387,	5605,	
		7484/7485	5611/5612	Red centre
		7497,	5624,	removed from
		7514/7515	5641/5642	US national
		7525,	5652,	insignia during
		7535,	5662,	6/42, affecting
		7539/7541	5666/5668	approximately
		7544,	5671,	last 50 P-38F-1s.
		7548/7550	5675/5677	
		7552/7680	5679/5807	
P-38F-5	100	42-12567/12666	7001/7100	6/42 and 7/42
F-5A-1 (P-38F-5)	20	12667/12686	7101/7120	6/42
P-38F-13	29	43-2035/2063	322-3144/3172	7/42
P-38F-15	121	2064/2184	3173/3293	8/42 and 9/42
P-38G-1	80	42-12687/12766	222-7121/7200	9/42
F-5A-3 (P-38G-3)	20	12767/12786	7201/7220	9/42
P-38G-3	12	12787/12798	7221/7232	9/42
P-38G-5	68	12799/12866	7233/7301	9/42 into 10/42
P-38G-10	97	12870/12966	7305/7401	10/42 into 11/42
F-5A-10 (P-38G-10)	20	12967/12986	7402/7421	11/42
P-38G-10	80	12987/13066	7422/7501	11/42 into 12/42
F-5A-10	60	13067/13126	7502/7561	12/42 into 1/43
P-38G-10	140	13127/13266	7562/7701	
F-5A-10	60	13267/13326	7702/7760	2/43
P-38G-10	231	13327/13557	7761/7991	1/43 into 2/43
P-38G-15	374	43-2185/2558	322-3294/3667	2/43 into 4/43
P-38H-1	226	42-13559,	222-1005,	4/43 into 6/43
		66502/66726	1013/1237	
P-38H-5	375	66727/67101	1238/1612	6/43 into 8/43 White bar added to US national insignia 7/43.
P-38J-1	10	12867/12869	422-1001/1003	8/43
		13560/13566	1006/1012	
P-38J-5	210	67102/67311	1613/1822	8/43 into 9/43
F-5B-1 (P-38J-5)	90	67312/67401	1823/1912	9/43 and 10/43
P-38J-10	790	67402/68191	1913/2702	10/43 into 12/43
F-5B-1 (P-38J-5)	110	68192/68301	2703/2812	12/43
P-38J-15	1,400	103979/104428	2813/3262	1/44 into 5/44
		43-28248/29047	3263/4062	
		44-23059/23208	4063/4212	
P-38J-20	350	23209/23558	4213/4562	5/44 into 6/44
P-38J-25	210	23559/23768	4563/4772	6/44
P-38K	(1)	Converted P-38E, s/n 41-1983		6/44
P-38L-1	1,291	42-13558	422-1004	6/44 into 9/44
		44-23769/25058	4773/6062	
P-38L-5	2,520	25059/27258	6063/8262	9/44 into 8/45
		53008/53327	8263/8582	
P-38L-5-VN	113	43-50339/52225	8583/9962	1/45 into 6/45
	10,036			

The following modifications are on record, although such a list is necessarily incomplete, and delivery dates from the mod centre at Dallas were not recorded. Individual aircraft record cards do show 'date received', but in the case of machines sent overseas this represented the shipping date. (The P-38M Night Fighter has shipping dates beginning 1 August 1945, so it appears unlikely that any Ms could have seen combat prior to the war's end.)

AF Model	Quantity		Approx Delivery Date
F-5C-1	128	Converted from P-38J-5	4/44 into 6/44
XF-5D	1	Converted from F-5A-10	
F-5E-2	100	Converted from P-38J-15	6/44 into 8/44
F-5E-3	105	Converted from P-38J-25	8/44 into 9/44
F-5E-4	508	Converted from P-38L-1	9/44 into 11/44
F-5F	unknown	Converted from P-38L-5	
F-5G	63	Converted from P-38L-5	1/45 into 3/43
FO-1	4	F-5A-1s transferred to US Navy in North Africa	
P-38M	75	Converted from P-38L-5	7/45 into 10/45